THÉÂTRE PROFANE

(seven plays)

Carleton Renaissance Plays in Translation No. 25

Series Editors: Donald Beecher, Douglas Campbell,
Massimo Ciavolella

Carleton Renaissance Plays in Translation

Marguerite of Angoulême
Duchess of Alençon and of Berri
Queen of Navarre

Théâtre Profane

Translated, with an Introduction and Notes, by

Régine Reynolds-Cornell

Dovehouse Editions Inc.
Ottawa
1992

Canadian Cataloguing in Publication Data

Marguerite, Queen, consort of Henry II, King of Navarre, 1492-1549

Théâtre profane

(Carleton Renaissance plays in translation ; 25
Translation of the work of the same title.
ISBN 1-895537-07-X (bound); 1-895537-06-1 (paper)

I. Reynolds-Cornell, Régine   II. Title.   III. Series.

PQ1631.A27 1992   842'.2   C92-090102-6

For information about the series:
   The Editors, Carleton Renaissance Plays in Translation
   Dept. of English
   Carleton University
   Ottawa, Ontario K1S 5B6

For distribution and ordering:
   Dovehouse Editions Inc.
   1890 Fairmeadow Cres.
   Ottawa, Canada K1H 7B9

Typeset in Canada

Dedication

In addition to John, Dennis and Eric, this is for two wonderfully young women: my dear friends Ilse Gaupp and Vivian Cornell, for their 90th and 99th birthdays respectively.

Table of Contents

Acknowledgments

I would like to express my thanks to the following persons: my colleagues at Agnes Scott College for their patience in answering numerous questions while I worked on this volume; my friend Oscar Bonner who read aloud my translation of each play; his encouragement was invaluable; our experts in academic computing who saved my sanity when the computer on which I typed this book was contaminated by an unmentionable virus; and the editors of this series for their most helpful comments and suggestions.

INTRODUCTION

1492, depending on which side of the Atlantic Ocean one resided, might be considered the glorious beginning of a new era, or the bearer of less-than-happy news. For Louise de Savoie, the fifteen-year-old wife of Charles d'Angoulême, "still childless" after three years of marriage, little mattered but a most desired event: the birth of her first child. Needless to say, she wanted a son, but little Marguerite was born in Angoulême, at 2:00 a.m. on Wednesday April 11th, 1492, a leap year.[1] The Journal in which Louise recorded all events that she considered of major importance—and we must admit that she most likely did so long after they had taken place—reveals that while she loved her daughter, it is the birth of her adored son François on Friday September 12th, 1494 that confirmed that fame would be theirs in her lifetime: "She had known it all along, it was in the stars."

Louise, intelligent and well-read, was also either very superstitious or wise enough to use to its full advantage the belief shared by many that the fate of special persons, particularly the highborn, resulted from divine intervention and was often revealed by "signs" such as comets or eclipses. As was the case for most princes and members of royal families, her horoscope and those of her children were drawn each year,[2] and her own physician-astrologer accompanied her in all official travels.

On January 1st, 1496—a leap year, she duly noted—Charles d'Angoulême died. At age nineteen,[3] Louise was a widow, and she promptly made plans for the future of her children, plans that clearly did not include living in Angoumois. Royal whims were in her favor: the king of France invited her and her offspring to move to the castle of Amboise, where they resided for about ten years. Louise understood the value of culture, but she showed remarkable foresight in engaging enlightened and dedicated scholars (Cop, Vatable and Hurault among others) for her children's education. Under their tutelage, Marguerite and her brother developed a deep love of learning and they gained an undeniable intellectual advantage over many members of the royal family. It is not my intention to present a thorough (and perhaps redundant) biography of Marguerite, but it seems important to mention the circumstances and some of the events that had a direct effect on her thought and more particularly on her writings.

At seventeen years of age, an unmarried lady of the aristocracy was considered a bit long in the tooth, but Marguerite, clearly enjoying life at court with her brother, did not seem to mind, although Louise—as she pointedly commented in her Journal— "had been left *all alone*" in Amboise. François had already been betrothed to the ten-year old Claude, daughter of King Louis XII,[4] for two years when, in its infinite wisdom, the Crown selected a spouse for Louise's intelligent, well-educated and charming (but certainly not beautiful) daughter. On December 2nd, 1509, a distraught Marguerite was thus married to Charles, Fourth Duke of Alençon, a kind man of limited intellect, perhaps even illiterate, whose widowed mother wore a nun's habit. Witnesses reported that during the wedding ceremony the bride "wept enough tears to hollow out a stone" (Elle pleurait à fendre le caillou).

Because her new residence had no library, the young Duchess of Alençon brought with her a large number of books; she also re-quested that all new publications of interest be routinely sent to her. We must in all fairness mention that Charles owned at least one book, *Le Nouvelin de la Vénerie*, a treatise on the raising and training of dogs for the hunt as well as the precise technique to work, run and force the stag. This splendidly illuminated manuscript bearing his arms may have been a gift. While she spent many a day reading "until her eyes could bear it no longer," Marguerite does not seem to have tried her hand at writing more than short poems and letters. Far from idle, she soon introduced culinary innovations in a kitchen where meals were abundant but taste was seen as a frivolous concession to pleasure. It is a matter of record that although numerous feasts and banquets took place in Alençon after her arrival—clearly at her initiative—she missed her friends and past companions, and that she pleaded with her brother to invite her to Normandy for at least a brief reunion. She never-theless enjoyed a pleasant relationship with her kind mother-in-law (who finally became a nun and died in a convent), and the Duke appears to have been a faithful—if boring—partner in a dull marriage. In a tale of the *Heptameron*, one of Marguerite's narrators explains that a woman had no children "because her head and her heart were somewhere else when she was in her husband's bed." For what this detail is worth, we should perhaps keep in mind that there was no hint of a pregnancy during the fifteen years of Marguerite's union with Charles.

In 1515, with the death of Louis XII, Louise's ambitions for her son were realized: against all odds, François acceded to the throne. As the King's sister, the duchess of Alençon returned to court life, journeying extensively for official visits to all provinces of the realm. It is perhaps then that she became aware of the dire need for reforms in convents and sought the advice of none other than a most respected humanist and scholar: Jacques Lefèvre d'Etaples. Their mutual support (his, spiritual, and hers, protection from his powerful enemies) lasted until his death in 1536.

1521 represents a turning point in Marguerite's spiritual itinerary. She must have sensed a lack of direction, a need for a stronger anchor in her religious life, and Lefèvre introduced her to the austere and much-admired Guillaume Briçonnet, Bishop of Meaux. Briçonnet sent her as spiritual counselor the soon-to-be controversial Michel d'Arande. He also pursued by correspondence with her an epistolary dialogue on religion and more particularly on the Scriptures. For a reader unfamiliar with obscure metaphors and exceedingly complex syntax, these letters may be described as taxing, but Marguerite, a diligent pupil, eagerly followed the religious path in which the Bishop of Meaux guided her.

The call for reform within the Roman Church found an increasingly receptive public in France, notably in Briçonnet's and Lefèvre's Evangelical Cenacle of Meaux. Marguerite read Luther's 95 Theses (posted four years earlier), as well as his other works published in 1520, for his words were fast spreading through most of Europe. As could be expected, the Faculty of Theology of the University of Paris[5] reacted with the utmost vigor: Luther was excommunicated and all his works were condemned.

In 1523, a large number of religious exegeses and treatises, including Melanchthon's and all of Berquin's, were condemned as "dangerous" and "heretical." Within a few years, the works of Erasmus, Lefèvre d'Etaples, Robert Estienne and of course those of Calvin were also blacklisted. Numerous books were burned in public in front of Notre-Dame Cathedral; the Meaux Cenacle would soon be dispersed.

1524 (a leap year, as Louise would probably remind us) was particularly painful for Marguerite: Philiberte of Savoy, her twenty-six-year-old aunt and close friend, died on April 4th. Claude, queen of France, died on July 24th, followed barely six weeks later by her little daughter Charlotte. Marguerite had returned to Blois to take care of her nieces and nephews during Claude's final illness, and she was deeply affected by the death of this child. Late that year or very early in 1525, she wrote the *Dialogue en Forme de Vision Nocturne*, an evangelical meditation in verse on death and redemption, in the form of a dialogue with little Charlotte. In this text, which she did not attempt to publish at the time,[6] one sees for the first time Marguerite's unwavering religious convictions, those to be found later in the *Mirror of the Sinful Soul*, in her *Théâtre Profane*, and in numerous works in verse, convictions that were greatly and boldly at odds with the teachings of the Roman Church. Soon after this, but obviously before February 24th, 1525, the date of the disaster of Pavia, she wrote the *Petit Oeuvre Dévot et Contemplatif*, also in verse, a treatise in which one recognizes more than a few of Briçonnet's metaphors, and in which one can appreciate how far she had strayed from traditional Roman teachings.

After Pavia, which left France without a king, followed by the death of her husband less than two months later, she undoubtedly had very little time to write: she travelled to Spain to obtain from Emperor Charles V the release of her brother, "whom she found near death." Humiliated and enraged after several meetings with the Emperor, she left Madrid for France in the dead of winter and crossed the Pyrenees on horseback at full speed under threat of becoming a prisoner herself.

Charles V wrote to the Regent Louise in 1526 to ask her for her daughter's hand in marriage for himself,[7] but the widowed Duchess of Alençon harbored such loathing for him that not even her brother could have coaxed her into accepting this union. She far preferred the young (her junior by eleven years), dashing and handsome Henri d'Albret, King of Navarre, whom she married in January 1527 in the castle of St Germain-en-Laye. She could have aspired to a more prestigious union, but she had earned the right to select the spouse of her choice, and the king raised no objection. That she loved Henri and remained faithful to him is quite certain; whether he loved her is debatable but likely. There is no doubt that he was deeply fond of her, but much enjoyed the company of attractive women. Marguerite analyzes the joys of love and the pain of jealousy too well not to have experienced them, and it is with great sensitivity that she studies the complexities of loyalty and betrayal in friendship and in marriage. It is, however, remarkable that she succeeded in expressing diverse masculine and feminine—occasionally controversial—views on this touchy subject in *The Coach*, the *Comedy for Four Women*, *On Perfect Love*, and of course in the revealing conversations among the narrators of *The Heptameron*.

Jeanne, her first child, was born in the castle of Fontainebleau on November 16th, 1528, but, loved as she may have been, she resided in Normandy during most of her childhood and does not seem to have spent much time with her mother. Marguerite's first priority was her brother, and, thus, her service to the French Crown, which was often at odds with her own interests as Queen of Navarre. She was also deeply involved in the protection of various scholars and poets: all was not well for those who challenged the teachings of the Roman Church. Clément Marot had been jailed in the infamous Châtelet in 1526; in spite of her pleas, another of her protégés, Berquin, author of *La manière de bien prier selon la doctrine évangélicque*, was burned at the stake in early 1529. A few months later, while she and Louise negotiated the terms of the Treaty of Cambrai (the Peace of the Ladies) with Margaret of Austria, Marguerite was, as Queen of Navarre, the "hostage" that would assure the safe return of the Emperor's aunt to Austria.[8]

Her first (and only) son Jean was born in Blois during the night of July 14th to 15th, 1530; Marguerite was then thirty-eight years old, middle-aged if not already old by sixteenth-century standards. Alas, the infant died on Christmas Day of the same year. Marguerite, Queen of Navarre, officially stated, "The Lord Giveth, The Lord Taketh Away," but Marguerite, grieving mother, confided to her friend George d'Armagnac (then Bishop of Rodez) that the death of this child weighed heavily on her heart and that she was finding it very difficult to cope with this loss.

She had reacted to the death of her niece Charlotte by composing the *Dialogue in the Form of a Nocturnal Vision*; after the death of this much-desired child, she coped again with her grief by writing the *Mirror of the Sinful Soul*, whose *editio princeps* was published in 1531 by Simon du Bois, in Alençon.[9] Both of these verse works, meditations on death and redemption, reveal Marguerite's depth of emotion and her more than passing acquaintance with Luther's writings. In fact, between 1526 and 1531 she wrote a translation of the Lord's Prayer; the *Mirror of the Sinful Soul*; a *Prayer to Our Lord Jesus*, a prose translation of the *Salve Regina*, a traditional invocation to the Virgin Mary, which she directed to the Christ; a *Prayer from the Faithful Soul*; and the *Discord between the Soul and the Flesh*, a commentary on Chapters VII and VIII of Paul's Epistle to the Romans. Few of these texts would have been appreciated by the increasingly suspicious Roman Church. The very old Lefèvre d'Etaples, who had survived exile and formal accusations of heresy, found himself in a precarious situation. Marguerite saw to it that he spent his last years in peace and out of harm's way in her castle of Nérac.

Louise died in 1531; the King keenly felt the loss of his doting mother, and for several years Marguerite—whose views on religion and whose choice of spiritual advisers could not fail to be (and were) noticed and criticized—stayed at Court as often and as long as she possibly could. In 1532, the year in which *Pantagruel* was published, she continued to protect "dangerous" poets such as Marot and numerous others whose religious writings were condemned as heretical by the Faculty of Theology of Paris.

In 1533, however, Marguerite must have felt surprisingly sure of herself and of her brother's protection: not only did she invite the controversial (evangelical) Gérard Roussel to give all the Sermons for Lent at the Louvre, but she also ordered that a second edition of her *Mirror of the Sinful Soul* be printed in Paris.[10] The *editio princeps* had been more or less unnoticed, but Marguerite daringly added to this work Marot's verse translation in French[11] of the Sixth Psalm and of six prayers: the *Pater Noster*, the *Ave Maria*, the *Credo*, the *Prayer of Blessings before a meal*, the *Graces for a Child*, and the *Dizain for an ailing Christian*. The *Miroir* was instantly condemned by the Faculty of Theology of Paris. That a religious meditation written by the Most Christian King's beloved sister should be placed on the list of forbidden, heretical texts likely to be burned in public seems paradoxical, if not highly comical, but François was not amused. On five different occasions, in October and November, the Sorbonne reluctantly retracted its condemnation of the *Miroir*, but it retaliated less than two years later with the hanging of Antoine Augereau, who had printed the offending and resented volume.

The spring of 1534 saw Calvin's anguished resignation from the Catholic pulpit, his somewhat hurried departure from Paris and, on his circuitous way to Basel, his stay at Marguerite's castle of Nérac, where he found solace conversing with Lefèvre and various evangelical scholars. Alas, the disastrous "Affaire des Placards" later that year was to seal the fate of many a Lutheran or evangelical proselytizer. When a procession was held in Paris and six "heretics" were burned at the stake on January 21st, 1535, Marguerite had already, perhaps at her brother's request or advice, left Court. Except for a brief visit in January 1537 to attend the marriage of her niece Madeleine to James of Scotland, she travelled extensively, but spent much time in Béarn, and did not reside at the Louvre until 1540. The British Ambassador wrote to his King that she was not likely ever to hold one-third of her former power with her brother.

Saulnier convincingly proves that it is in 1535 that she wrote *The Patient and the Cure*. Having left Paris, spending several months at a time in Pau, she must have found more time to read and write. She also fervently hoped for a reconciliation between the Roman Church and those that it considered dissidents, if not enemies. But she spent most of 1536, the year in which she wrote her satirical *Inquisitor*, in Lyons, a city where the mood was quite different from that of Paris. There, Maurice Scève and Etienne Dolet were introduced to her, she engaged Bonaventure des Périers as her "Valet de chambre," Marot rejoined her entourage upon his return from exile, and she met or renewed acquaintance with various authors and printers. Although this cannot be proven, she was probably (and so was Marot) one of the authors of Madame Jeanne Flore's *Contes Amoureux*, written in that city in 1536.[12] The Roman Church complained that she was "still accompanied by her Lutheran demons under the name of advisers."

Bonaventure des Périers, whose *Cymbalum Mundi* had created a scandal in 1538, committed suicide in 1540. It was also the year of the marriage contract between Jeanne d'Albret and the Duke of Clèves, a union imposed by the King against the will of both mother and daughter. That year and the next, Marguerite wrote *La Coche*, *Le triumphe de l'aigneau*, and various poems of religious inspiration.

Her *Comedy for Four Women*, which is in fact a play with ten characters very much anticipating the narrators of the *Heptameron*, was probably written around January 1542, since it was performed in February of that year.[13]

In late 1544 or early 1545, she wrote *Most, Much, Little, Less*, and this play, sharply critical of the Roman Church, reveals that she no longer believed in a reconciliation between the Sorbonne authorities and the followers of the (by then dispersed) Cenacle of Meaux. 1545 is also the year during which she broke all relations with Calvin, who had become increasingly critical of her and more particularly of those "Sectaires" (already accused of heterodoxy by the Faculty of Theology of Paris) whom she protected. There were however some compensations: the Pope's annulment of Jeanne's marriage to the Duke of Clèves gave Marguerite and Henri new hope for their long-cherished plan to marry their daughter to Philip of Spain,[14] and the Council of Trent—in which she placed great hopes for a peaceful solution to the religious discord—held at long last its first meeting.

In spite of the publication of Rabelais's *Tiers Livre*, which was dedicated to her, 1546 was a bitter year for Marguerite. Her daughter was forbidden to leave France for Navarre; her husband's young mistress had given him a son; and, sorrow of sorrows, she felt consistently more isolated and almost alienated from her brother. She had returned to Pau after the Massacre des Vaudois; it is well known that when Meynier d'Oppède's son-in-law spoke before the King's Council in an attempt to justify the massacre, Marguerite was so incensed that she never looked in his direction, thus forcing him to stay on his knees during his entire speech; she clearly understood that those responsible would never be punished and that, while she could express her indignation, she was powerless to act.[15] Privately, as a wife, mother, and sister, as well as politically, her star was waning. Etienne Dolet, another of her protégés, was burned at the stake in Paris. Lefèvre, Berquin, Briçonnet, des Périers, Marot, all were dead.

At this point, her thoughts must have turned to her own death and to her accomplishments in her lifetime. She must have reached the conclusion that some of her writings were worthy of being printed, and proceeded to an edition of those that she had selected. The title that she chose, *Les Marguerites de la Marguerite des*

Princesses, Tresillustre Royne de Navarre (Flowers—or pearls—of the Pearl Among Princesses), was an obvious play on the Latin word "margarita," which means both a pearl and a daisy, as well as her own name, but not altogether an exercise in humility.

In this elegant volume printed in Lyons in 1547 by Jean de Tournes,[16] we find the *Dialogue in the form of a Nocturnal Vision*; *The Mirror of the Sinful Soul* with the addenda of its second edition; *The Triumph of the Lamb of God* (Le Triumphe de l'Aigneau); *Complaint for One Held Prisoner* (Complainte pour Un Détenu Prisonnier);[17] various epistles in verse, numerous poems, some bucolic, others addressed to her brother; a few religious meditations; four *Mystères* most likely written after 1535; *The Coach* (La Coche). Of the seven plays translated in the present volume, two farces were prudently omitted: *The Patient and the Cure* and of course *The Inquisitor*; the last two (*Comedy of Mont de Marsan* and *Comedy On Perfect Love*) had not yet been written. The *Marguerites* also included most of her *Chansons Spirituelles*, where she uses the *Contrefactum*, a popular late medieval genre in which new lyrics, in this case devout, are substituted for those of well-known (and sometimes very naughty) songs.[18]

It has not been sufficiently stressed that she seems to have deliberately and most carefully chosen for this, her own monument for posterity, an example of each of the literary genres that she had used. We may therefore assume that in doing so she wanted to prove her versatility, if not the originality of her creations. This meticulous selection points to her desire to present her works as those of a serious author and to lift the mask of dilettante that, as a member of royalty, she had insisted on wearing.

In March of 1547, having—at his request—begun the long journey to Paris to join her gravely ill brother, she stopped in Tusson, slightly beyond the half-way mark. There she was to learn of the King's death, which the nuns were desperately trying to hide from her. Devastated by what was perhaps the most cruel loss in her life, she remained at the convent until August, writing *The Sailing Ship* (La Navire), before returning to Béarn. If she was then writing *Prisons* (Les Prisons), this jewel in her crown was obviously not completed, for she would undoubtedly have included it when she published her *Marguerites*: it represents the culmination of her literary career.[19]

In early 1548, she left Pau for Mont de Marsan, where she remained until late April, writing the *Comedy on the Passing of the King* (Comédie sur le Trespas du Roy). On October 20th of that year, in Moulins, she was seen weeping at the marriage of her daughter to Antoine of Bourbon-Vendôme. Not only was Henri of Navarre's and Marguerite's dream of a union with Philip of Spain shattered, but they were treated with much condescension by those who wanted to please the new king. Marguerite knew that this was her last voyage to the court where, as her brother's "mignonne," she had lived as a queen, and she may have been quite ready emotionally to accept her new status as an expendable parent. She gave no hint of her disappointment in the *Heptameron*: in the sixty-sixth tale, we are told of an old chambermaid who, thinking that she had caught a guest in bed with a young lady of the household, burst into Jeanne and Antoine de Bourbon's room soon after their wedding and insulted them, to their great amusement.

A few months later, in 1549, expecting a visit from Jeanne and Antoine, she wrote her brief comedy *On Perfect Love* (Le Parfait Amant). She was still working on her planned "*Decameron*," various chansons and poems, and most likely put the final touches on *Prisons*. In early December of that year, Henri of Navarre was summoned by Henri II, the new King of France, to join him at court. Immediately upon his arrival in Paris he was informed of his wife's illness and left at once. He must have travelled at breakneck speed, for he reached the Castle of Odos on December 21st, barely a few hours after Marguerite's death.[20]

Except for her posthumous *Heptameron*, undoubtedly the most scrutinized of her works, her literary legacy remained unfairly ignored until the end of the last century, and she was generally considered a very minor, negligible and exceedingly garrulous writer. Although her reputation as a gifted and most influential author has steadily grown among scholars and graduate students, she is still occasionally "miscast" as a Spanish member of royalty,[21] or as her nephew's daughter Marguerite, la reine Margot.

One cannot deny that the plays in her *Théâtre Profane* are uneven, but we should keep in mind that—except in the case of the *Comedy on the Passing of the King* and the *Comedy of Mont de Marsan*—she thought of her theater as a casual and pleasing form of entertainment for noble guests, or as proselytizing plays that could safely be performed at her own court, and which she called "farces."

Farces were certainly not seen as a noble genre: they were generally offered as preludes or as entertaining interludes between more important performances, such as *mystères*. Most farces were brief (400 lines or less, a limit that Marguerite consistently overlooked), and were seldom, if at all, divided into acts and scenes. The meter, usually octosyllabic, was occasionally pentasyllablic, and Marguerite did not hesitate to blend both in the same play. The characters were identified by their clothing, their occupation, or their age rather than by subtle hints, and, needless to say, there was very little preamble to the action, another rule that Marguerite chose to ignore.

In her three "farces" on religion, she satirized the clergy, a frequent and quite popular *topos* of the medieval farce, but her satire (which pointedly avoided easy jokes on gluttony, ribaldry and debauch) was part of a more noble aim, spurred by her altruistic desire to proselytize. In the medieval farce, laughter took precedence over the moral message if there was one at all, but in Marguerite's, the message is clearly expressed and readily understood by the audience, particularly that of her entourage, although it is not always grasped or accepted by the protagonists. Among her satirical plays, *The Inquisitor*, and *Most, Much, Little, Less*, two excellent exempla of the rhetoric of pragmatic silence, are true admonitions to discretion and prudence.

In the comedy, on the other hand, the moral message had or was expected to have precedence over laughter. Marguerite's plays on the *topos* of love do praise patience, virtue, loyalty, and faithfulness, and they allow occasional laughter. Her comedies on religion, and particularly those on death and redemption, leave no room for levity, although examples of *sub rosa* humor and irony interspersed in the *Comedy of Mont de Marsan* cannot fail to bring about a smile if not a chuckle. She seems to have enjoyed experimenting with meter, which reveals much diversity: decasyllabic, octosyllabic, pentasyllabic lines are all found in three of the comedies, while the last is entirely decasyllabic.

A brief analysis will precede each of the translated plays—for which I used V.L. Saulnier's 1963 revised edition of the *Théâtre Profane*.[22] Translating verse from French to English is a time-consuming and frustrating task, for the risk of betraying the original text in content or in style is real and constant. Syllabic count is an arduous task in English, but in this text it must parallel that of the original French, for the simple and obvious reason that it reflects the personality and the speech pattern of each character. Rhyme and rhythm are elusive, and I often felt compelled to sacrifice rhyme for the sake of meaning or cadence. Except in rare cases of comic repetition that could be neither omitted nor modified, I attempted to respect the traditional patterns used by Marguerite, and the critical reader will find in my text true rhymes, an occasional "rime riche," numerous visual rhymes, certainly off-rhymes, and perhaps a few macaronic rhymes (of which Marguerite was sometimes guilty herself), for which I beg indulgence.

In view of the fact that Marguerite's French was that of an educated woman of the sixteenth century, a deliberate effort was made to avoid all modern American structures and idioms. My somewhat "quaint" English seems to echo the tone and the mood of the plays better than a more casual and colloquial English. Furthermore, great care was taken in translating those numerous words whose meanings have substantially changed over the centuries, in English as well as in French. When old proverbs (whole or in part) and idiomatic expressions defied translation or appeared meaningless in a modern context, they were given an approximate equivalent. Deliberate ambiguity as a frequent rhetorical device was respected, for obvious reasons. Malapropisms, awkwardness of style or of speech in the original text were duplicated as scrupulously as possible, yet I may have unwittingly produced a few of my own.

All notes, whether historical or lexical, were included whenever it was felt that they would lead to a better comprehension or appreciation of the text. Due credit has been given to V.L. Saulnier whenever I quoted or adapted notes from his 1963 edition.

NOTES TO THE INTRODUCTION

1. Louise and her offspring have been the subject of numerous studies. On Marguerite alone, we can name the excellent studies by Pierre Jourda, Abel Lefranc, Marcel Bataillon, V.L. Saulnier, Ph.A. Becker, Felix Frank, M. de la Ferrière-Percy, Michel Dassonville, R. Marichal, Robert Aulotte, François Rigolot, Robert Cottrell, and Marcel Tetel. Among biographies one must note those by Martha Walker Freer, 1898; Marie-Jeanne Darmesteter, 1900; Pierre Jourda, 1930; Samuel Putnam, 1935; and Paul Ricoeur's beautiful work on "The Queen of Navarre's Solitudes." My own biography of Marguerite (1980), *Marguerite d'Angoulême, Duchess of Alençon, Queen of Navarre, a Tryptych*, presenting the public, the private and the secret person as three distinctentities, deliberately played havoc with chronology and remains unpublished.

2. Bibliotheque Nationale, Ms fr. 2082.

3. Louise was born, she tells us, *at 5:24 P.M.* on September 11th, 1476, a leap year.

4. An Italian ambassador reported that the young Princess engaged to the "healthy and handsome" François "limped on both legs." We must assume that Claude suffered from a congenital hip disorder caused by or related to the tuberculosis of which she was to die after giving birth to seven children between August 1515 and June 1523. Louise and Charlotte died before the age of 10 (the former was 2 and the latter 7), Madeleine and François before they were 18, Charles at 23. Henri, who acceded to the throne in 1547, and Marguerite are the only two who enjoyed healthy lives. Henri was 40 when he was mortally wounded, and his sister Marguerite lived to the ripe age of 51.

5. As James K. Farge has clearly shown in his *Index de l'Université de Paris, Index des Livres Interdits*, published by the Centre d'Etudes de la Renaissance, there was an overlap of judicial functions, but those of the Bishops and those of the Faculty were different, and the judicial branch of the University of Paris was not officially called the Sorbonne.

6. This first known work of hers was not published until 1533, when she commissioned Simon du Bois, of Alençon, to print it.

7. Bibliothèque Nationale, Paris, MS. Béthune 8496, folio 13.

8. According to the terms of this treaty, the young French Princes—then held in Spain in exchange for their father's freedom—would return to France with the Emperor's sister Eleanor, Queen of Portugal, and

bride-to-be of the French King. François was to relinquish (but did not) claims on various territories.

9.   Bibliothèque Nationale, in-quarto, Y 4369 Réserve.
       Ann Boleyn, who had been one of Marguerite's ladies in waiting, owned a copy of the *Miroir de l'Ame Pécheresse*. Her daughter Elizabeth, future Queen of England, later translated this work into English for her stepmother Catherine Parr's birthday.

10.   *Le Miroir de Tres Chrestienne Princesse Marguerite de France, Royne de Navarre, Duchesse d'Alençon & de Berry / auquel elle voit son néant & son tout.* Bibliothèque Nationale, Y 4525.

11.   Cf. Royal Edict of February 3rd, 1526: "It is forbidden to all persons to recite, display or translate from Latin into French the Epistles of Saint-Paul, the Book of the Apocalypse or any other Book of the Scriptures, and to speak of the Ordinance of the Church, or of the Images in any manner except those decreed by the Holy Church from its earliest times."

12.   Cf. my article (soon to be followed by a sequel), "Madame Jeanne Flore and the *Contes Amoureux*: A Pseudonym and a Paradox," in *Bibliothèque d'Humanisme et Renaissance*, LI, No. 1 (1989), 123-33.

13.   Saulnier provides the reference for the letter sent to Henri VIII by William Paget, British Ambassador to France, on February 26th, 1542, mentioning this play, "which was performed by the King's daughter, Madame d'Etampes, Madame de Nevers, Madame Montpensier and Madame Bellay": State Papers, 1849, Vol. VIII, p. 667.

14.   They soon realized that the King of France would never give his approval to such a marriage. When they left the Court to return to Pau, François gave strict orders that Jeanne be closely watched to prevent her leaving with her parents.

15.   The Vaudois were not disciples of Luther or of Calvin. They only accepted the Old and the New Testament, refused every form of dogma of the Roman Church, and were excommunicated by the Pope in the twelfth century. Their way of life differed sensibly from that of the Cathares, and could easily be compared to that of the Evangelicals of the sixteenth century. In three days, about three thousand men, women and children according to a Protestant source, several hundred according to a Catholic report, were massacred. 763 houses, 89 cattle sheds and 31 granaries were burned to the ground; three small towns and 22 villages were sacked. Of those who survived and were captured, more than 600 were sent to the galleys and 255 were executed after being tried. Children were sold into some form of slavery, and it was

forbidden, under threat of death, to provide food or shelter to any of the Vaudois. Those who had succeeded in escaping founded congregations in France, Switzerland and Italy, among other areas.

16.   A few copies were found in which both sections were bound into a single volume; others were in two separate tomes.

17.   A few scholars have suggested that this unknown man kept prisoner was the King of France himself; most others, with whom I agree, feel that it was most likely Clément Marot.

18.   It goes without saying that these songs were not heard in the Roman Church. They were, however, well known; several of them became most popular and were sung by Huguenot congregations.

19.   This long poem (6,000 lines) remained unknown until 1898. It is divided into three parts representing the three temptations in the author's life: that of love (about 1,000 lines), followed by ambition and the enjoyment of fame and honors (about 2,000 lines), and finally the fascination with books and the study of the Scriptures (about 3,000 lines), leading to a sort of mystical ecstasy. It is undoubtedly her best and most polished work, and it has recently been translated.

20.   It took a courier two days to gallop from Paris to Orleans and twelve days from Paris to Marseille, a slightly shorter distance than from Paris to Odos. Montaigne mentions his post-haste journey from the Italian border to Bordeaux lasting "more than three weeks."

21.   The Editor of Yale University Press sent me the following letter on August 24, 1979: "Thank you for telling us of your manuscript: *Marguerite d'Angoulême, Duchess of Alençon and Queen of Navarre: A Triptych.* Although it sounds most interesting from your description, we publish so little in Spanish History that I do not think we would be the best house for this book. I wish you good luck in placing the manuscript."

22.   *Marguerite de Navarre: Théâtre Profane.* Première publication collective par V.L. Saulnier, Professeur à la Sorbonne. Nouvelle Edition Revue. *Textes Littéraires Français.* Geneva: Droz, 1963.

SELECTED BIBLIOGRAPHY

Ames, Sanford S. "A Severe and Militant Charity." *L'Esprit Createur* 28, 2 (1988): 89-95.

Bernard, John D. "Realism and Closure in the *Heptameron*: Marguerite and Boccaccio." *Modern Language Review* 84, 2 (1989): 305-18.

Bowen, Barbara. *Words and the Man in French Renaissance Literature*. Lexington: French Forum, 1983.

Cholakian, Patricia Francis. *Rape and Writing in the "Heptameron" of Marguerite de Navarre*. Carbondale: Southern Illinois University Press, 1991.

Cottrell, Robert. *The Grammar of Silence: A Reading of Marguerite de Navarre's Poetry*. Washington: Catholic University Press, 1986.

Davis, Natalie Zemon. *Fiction in the Archives: Pardon Tales and their Tellers in Sixteenth-Century France*. Stanford: Stanford University Press, 1987.

Farge, James K. *Orthodoxy and Reform in Early Reformation France: The Faculty of Theology of Paris, 1500-1543*. Leiden, 1985.

Gelernt, Jules. *World of Many Loves: The Heptameron of Marguerite de Navarre*. Chapel Hill: University of North Carolina, 1966.

Hauser, Henri. "Le Journal de Louise de Savoie." *Revue Historique* LXXXVI. Nogent, 1904.

Heller, Henry. *Marguerite de Navarre and the Reformers of Meaux*. Geneva: Bibliothèque d'Humanisme et Renaissance, XXXIII, 1971.

Jourda, Pierre. *Marguerite d'Angoulême*. Paris: Bibliothèque litteraire de la Renaissance, 1930.

Kingdon, Robert M. "Problems of Religious Choice for Sixteenth-Century Frenchmen." *Journal of Religious History* 4 (1967): 105-12.

Lefevre d'Etaples, Jacques. *Epistres & Evangiles pour les Cinquante & Deux Sepmaines de l'An*. Facsimile edition with introduction and notes by M.A. Screech. Geneva: Droz, 1964.

Lefranc, Abel. *Marguerite de Navarre et le Platonisme de la Renaissance*. Grands Ecrivains Français de la Renaissance. Paris: Champion, 1914.

Linder, Robert D. "The Early Calvinists and Martin Luther: A Study in Evangelical Solidarity," in *Regnum, Religio et Ratio*, Essays presented to Robert M. Kingdon. *Sixteenth Century Essays & Studies*, VIII (1984): 103-16.

Prescott, Anne Lake. *The Pearl of the Valois and Elizabeth I: Marguerite de Navarre's "Miroir" and Tudor England*. *Silent but for the Word*, edited by Margaret P. Hannay. Kent, Ohio: Kent State University Press, 1985.

Reynolds-Cornell, Régine. "Silence as a Rhetorical Device in Marguerite de Navarre's *Théâtre Profane*." *The Sixteenth Century Journal* XVII (Spring 1986): 17-32.

Roelker, Nancy. "The Appeal of Calvinism to French Noblewomen in the Sixteenth Century." *Journal of Interdisciplinary History* 2 (1972): 391-418.

Sommers, Paula. "The Mirror and its Reflections: Marguerite de Navarre's Biblical Feminism." *Tulsa Studies in Women's Literature*, Vol. 5, Spring 1986.

Stone, Donald. *France in the Sixteenth Century: A Medieval Society Transformed*. Englewood Cliffs: Prentice Hall, 1969.

Wilson, Katharina M. *Women Writers of the Renaissance and Reformation*. Athens: University of Georgia Press, 1987.

THE PATIENT AND THE CURE

(Le malade)

INTRODUCTION

Synopsis

A man, racked with a most painful ailment for which his kind wife suggests all sorts of remedies, asks for a doctor. While the good woman is on her way to fetch the physician, the servant girl reveals to the patient the secret of all health: God is the only way to salvation. Upon his arrival, the baffled doctor fails to understand how and why his patient appears rested and healthy, but nevertheless prescribes a remedy. He writes most precisely what must be done to the then-reluctant patient, but while he is absorbed in writing his prescription, the very simple evangelical message from the servant brings about a miraculous and instantaneous cure by conversion. The doctor, seeing that his services are no longer needed, accuses the girl of witchcraft and the wife of ill-advised and ignorant old wive's cures. Before leaving, he pockets his fee but offers his help if his client should relapse, and the play ends with the former patient's joyful paean to God.

History and Comments

V.L. Saulnier established that 1531 was the earliest and November 1543 the latest possible date for the composition of this "farce," and suggests 1535, the most logical choice, as its actual date. At that time, Marguerite still hoped for a peaceful solution to the internal problems of the Roman Church, which she wanted to nudge in the direction of the much-needed reforms that it resisted. As Saulnier indicated, she developed this play on a *topos* with which Briçonnet and numerous others were only too familiar: the distance and isolation of the clergy from its calling. Marguerite suggests that those of the Church who have the knowledge to share the Word do not necessarily have the wisdom or the compassion to do so, perhaps because written words and tradition have dimmed their eyes to the Light. The humble, the uncultured, may be closer to God because their faith is simple and sincere.

The character of the patient, in whom Saulnier saw the soul corrupted by sin, could also represent the ailing Church that has strayed from Grace and, though aware of its illness, is unable to identify it, and thus needs divine help in order to be cured. The doctor, whom the patient tellingly calls "Father" when he awakens him, insists on an age-old remedy (bleeding), but does not rely on the Book of Science (the Bible), and demands that *his* written prescription be strictly obeyed. Repeating or copying what he has learned from other men, he is neither devious nor evil, but he simply cannot cure a spiritual illness. Convinced that only he can save the patient, he calls "devilish" any cure for his patient but his own. Needless to say, he represents the dogmatic theologians and exegetes who fiercely cling to tradition and have lost touch with the simplicity of Faith, thus losing the way to the Good Doctor, God.

In spite of the fact that the remedy may be worse than the illness, the kind and concerned wife of the patient is willing to try every earthly cure recommended by well-meaning but misguided neighbors and friends. She also believes in all honesty that to obey God's command is to say one's prayers daily and to have masses sung for one's salvation. She insists that, having read two books, she cannot be called ignorant, and it is quite clear that she cannot establish a distinction between the word and the spirit. In other words, she represents the masses of sincere believers who place their entire trust in mechanical prayers and in the impressive but empty practices of the Church.

We should stress at this point that none of these three characters is accused of evil-doing or condemned for sin or ignorance: all three mean well. Overly concerned with earthly preoccupations and cares, they simply have not yet found the Way.

The maid represents, as does many a servant girl seen in popular comedies for centuries, and particularly in Molière's plays, the recognizable stereotype of an outspoken, no-nonsense, devoted member of the family. She also symbolizes here the unspoiled, child-like quality of those who possess the inestimable gift of true Faith, and thus the true power to lead others on the way to salvation.

At this point, it is to Lefèvre d'Etaples and no longer to Briçonnet that we should turn. Marguerite's old friend and spiritual guide had written, "To inherit the Kingdom of God, all you need is faith. With faith, nothing is impossible." He further explained that the Christian must prepare himself for justification, which requires prevenient grace (Gratia praeveniens), a call from God, which may be through the Scriptures or through divine inspiration, followed by exciting and assisting grace (Gratia excitans atque adjuvans), helping the Christian to turn his soul toward God, finally culminating in the free and joyful acceptance and cooperation with divine grace (Libere assentiendo et cooperando).

Lefèvre's text was, needless to say, among the many black-listed by the Sorbonne.[1] We should perhaps refrain from sarcasm when we note than on January 13th, 1547, the Council of Trent approved this very interpretation of the New Testament.

In this play, her first attempt at what I would call "non-biblical drama,"[2] Marguerite transposes with remarkable skill this process of conversion and of redemption from the abstract to the very visual and direct medium of the stage. The "malade," pleading for help, eagerly prepares himself, receives the Word, is converted and finally exults in full cooperation with divine grace. Given from the pulpit, and particularly when delivered in Latin, this message might not be understood by the faithful. Presented simply, in French, and acted in the familiar setting of a house where "real" people live, it becomes clear and easily accessible to the audience. The well-tried and proven principle of medieval *mystères* performed in churches for the edification of the flock is thus applied to everyday life, and the very human desire for salvation is addressed in terms that common people can understand.

It is undeniable that this play, far from a casual and idle choice on Marguerite's part, was a rational and very pragmatic answer to the nagging problem of reaching the faithful beyond the rigid barrier of dogma. She found comedy to be a practical and effective vehicle for her didactic but more purely proselytizing aim in this, as in every other play written on a religious theme. Echoing the devisants of her *Heptameron*—whose animated conversations are, basically, dramatic scenes on an open stage[3]—each of her characters embodies a viewpoint or an attitude and communicates to the spectators a message that can easily be grasped if they wish to do so.

There is no absolute proof that *The Patient and the Cure* was ever performed, but Saulnier indicates that stage directions were penned in the margin of the manuscript (preceding lines 161, 177, 193, 329). This too-rare example of technical detail provides us with a solid clue that the play was at least rehearsed by Marguerite's entourage.

The Patient and the Cure is in fact an original variation on a morality play. This early effort shows promise and is entertaining. However, without attempting to be overly critical, one should admit that there is much room for improvement. In its early stages, Marguerite's process of construction for her farces and comedies remains at the most basic level: the somewhat one-dimensional characters tell the audience where they are and what they are doing. Moreover, Marguerite's singleness of purpose overshadows the action one expects from a farce: the author has not yet learned how to disappear behind her characters, but she is clearly on the right track. Some of the gestures of the characters through the dialogue reveal a fine sense of the comic. From here on, each new play will show her honing her skill as a playwright and mastering the craft.

As most authors do when they re-read their early works, she must have noticed the weaknesses of this play when (around 1546) she selected her works for the *Marguerites de la Marguerite des Princesses* published in Lyons by Jean de Tourncs in 1547. While the most elementary prudence demanded that *The Inquisitor* be omitted from this miscellany, the evangelical message of *The Patient and the Cure* neither attacked nor did it ridicule (a far more dangerous crime!) the Faculty of Theology of the University of Paris, whose long-smoldering resentment could easily be fanned into a full-blown and vengeful fire. Yet, Marguerite chose not to include this play in her *Marguerites*. Caution may have motivated her, but by 1546 she was a more seasoned playwright; viewing her play critically, she was bound to sense, as we shall soon do, that her later proselytizing works were far superior. It is most fortunate that the only known copy of this text was found in a manuscript of the Bibliothèque Nationale (ms. fr. 12485), and meticulously edited by the late V.L. Saulnier. Indeed, this comedy represents a much-needed stepping stone, not only in the study of Marguerite's *Theater*, but because it represents her first attempt at proselytism through the medium of satirical comedy in the context of her opus as a whole.

THE PATIENT AND THE CURE

(Le malade)[4]

The Patient   His wife
The Maidservant   The Physician

SCENE I

PATIENT, WIFE.

PATIENT:	Dear wife, I feel terribly ill!
	My mouth is bitter, my heart faint,
	And in my side I have much pain.
WIFE:	One can see that you have grown pale.
	But please try to be of good cheer 5
	And force yourself to have a meal.
PATIENT:	Eat, when my life has lost savor?
	Eat, you say? You make me angry.
	Eat? I can assure you, my dear,
	That I have lost all appetite, 10
	And I could not swallow a bite,
	Small and tasty as it might be.
WIFE:	Then you must go to bed, my dear;
	There you will rest comfortably.
PATIENT:	Since nothing can give me pleasure, 15
	Like it or not, here I will stay.
WIFE:	And where is this pain that you feel?
PATIENT:	On the right side, below the breast,
	And I have in me such a thirst
	That nothing could make me feel worse.[5] 20
WIFE:	The white tooth of a boar to wear
	I shall give you, 'tis my custom,
	And of an herb that I know well
	I shall make you a cataplume.[6]

PATIENT:

Dear one, this cannot be the way   25
By which my illness can be cured.
Go presently, do not tarry,
And fetch me a skilled physician.

WIFE:

Why must you always run to them?
I find their paw too dangerous: 30
The other day they caused the death
Of the procultress's daughter.[7]
Between us, we humble women
Have knowledge from experience,
And upon my conscience, we know   35
Herbs and weeds as well as they do.
Do you think that all their science
Grants them the knowledge of all things?

PATIENT:

Go on, I am losing patience!
Leave at once, do your very best!   40

WIFE:

Very well, then, I shall fetch him,
Since you want him and no other.
But in the name of St. Peter,
I wish that you would change your mind.
If only you agreed to drink   45
The yolks of five eggs newly laid,
Your whole complexion would be changed
And you would be cured in a wink.[8]
But there I go, be satisfied.
If need be, I shall even run.   50

SCENE II

PATIENT, MAIDSERVANT.

PATIENT:

God help me, what am I to do?
This pain will be the death of me.
I cannot bear any longer
This forever worse affliction.
Of this world I shall not be long.   55
What is, my child, your opinion?[9]

MAIDSERVANT: If I dared, Master, tell the truth,
              And it pleased you to accept it,
              Your suffering would end forsooth;
              A doctor would not be needed.   60
PATIENT: I don't know to which Saint to turn,
              And thus I supplicate them all.[10]
MAIDSERVANT: By one only can you be cured,
              The only one worthy of praise.
PATIENT: Who has the power, as you claim,   65
              To deliver me from my pain?
MAIDSERVANT: It is He who, if you knew Him,
              Would make all your travails worthwhile.
              You would be deceived no longer
              By the cunning of false healers.   70
              But you would, with Him by your side,
              Challenge the illness and its woes.
PATIENT: Who is this Saint? Who can He be?
              I beg of you, name Him to me!
MAIDSERVANT: The Saint of Saints, the Great Master,[11]   75
              Who sanctifies Popes and Rulers,
              Is God. And I truly believe
              That He will cure you of your ills
              When at last, secure in your faith,
              You give to Him your whole being.   80
                  Can there be a wiser doctor
              Than is God, better, or kinder,
              More powerful—Can you hear me?
              And who could so love humankind
              That for you He suffered such woes   85
              And even death to make you whole,
              Snatching your soul away from wolves
              To take it unto His bosom?[12]
                  If you go to Him directly
              To tell Him your wretched story,   90
              And if you speak to Him freely
              As any good Christian should do,
              You will at once feel delivered
              From the bonds in which you suffered.[13]
              And if He should ignore your plea,   95

Lay your suffering at His feet.
 If you weighed, sitting in judgment,
Your human virtue and your sins,
You would deem insignificant
Your desolation and your pains.   100
You must accept and understand
That your wretched lot on this earth
Is nought but anguish and torment,
And that your sins make you evil.
 But if in total submission   105
You humbly atoned for your sins,
You would be cleansed from them
By divine and merciful Grace
That from the darkest depths of Hell
Can lift up the mortified soul,   110
Making it resplendent and pure,
Cleansed and delivered from all sins.
 Surrender unto Him now,
Master, your pleasure and your will!

PATIENT: I comprehend in all good faith   115
That God alone may grant us health.
Listening to you speak of Him
Made my heart rejoice so fully
That I felt suddenly relieved
From the ill that tormented me.   120
But upon such sweet discourse
It is time for me to repose.

SCENE III

WIFE, DOCTOR.

WIFE: Dear Sir, I came here to explain
That my husband is in much pain.
I dare not say how bad it is: 125
Do come look at him, if you please!

DOCTOR: But to help me treat this case,

<table>
<tr><td></td><td>You must tell me a thing or two;</td><td></td></tr>
<tr><td></td><td>My dear woman, I need to know</td><td></td></tr>
<tr><td></td><td>Where the pain is.</td><td></td></tr>
<tr><td>WIFE:</td><td>Under his breast.</td><td>130</td></tr>
<tr><td>DOCTOR:</td><td>When did it begin?</td><td></td></tr>
<tr><td>WIFE:</td><td>Yesterday,</td><td></td></tr>
</table>

WIFE: Under his breast.   130

DOCTOR: When did it begin?

WIFE: Yesterday,
But he said nought until today.
I know that you are a scholar,
And that you know Latin, my Lord,
But Fat Kate told me recently   135
  Of an excellent remedy:
  Of a white pigeon the droppings
  Daintily crushed, Sir, in a brew,
Would not even cost a farthing,
And could do no harm, I tell you![14]   140

DOCTOR: By my faith, you are no wiser
Than your meddlesome adviser,
For this cure, even in a broth,
Is forbidden in Languedoc.
  But let us be on our way;   145
I shall promptly give him a cure,
But first I need to look at him,
Then I shall decide on his case.
But I shall remain on my guard
That you and others don't intrude: 150
For if you do I shall depart,
Washing my hands of him and you.[15]

SCENE IV

WIFE, MAIDSERVANT, DOCTOR.

WIFE: Here we are, dear Sir, do come in.
  Girl! What is my husband doing?

MAIDSERVANT: He has been asleep since you left,   155
And had no complaint whatever.

WIFE: It would be the best remedy

	If he could rest in this manner.	
DOCTOR:	All this talk here is wasting time,	
	I must feel his pulse. Let's enter.	160

SCENE V

PATIENT, DOCTOR, WIFE, MAIDSERVANT.

(The doctor checks the man's pulse and wakes him up.)

PATIENT:	Who is this?	
DOCTOR:	It is I, my friend;	
	I have come to restore your health.	
PATIENT:	Ah, I had not seen you, father!	
	Be kind enough to forgive me.	
	I feel again the wretched pain	165
	That had deprived me of my rest.[16]	
	In one place I cannot remain,	
	And seem condemned to moan and sweat.	
DOCTOR:	My friend, we shall soon recover,	
	And we shall suffer no longer.	170
	Have you eaten of a pumpkin	
	Grown too close to iron or tin?[17]	
	Could your horse have too much spirit?	
	Were you in much cold or drizzle?	

(He turns to the wife.)

	You there, bring me this urinal.	175
	I must see if all is normal.	

(He examines the urinal, and speaks.)

	Truly we are doing better	
	Than I thought, friend, or than I feared.	
	Our urine is pure and our eyes	
	Quite clear. In other words, frankly,	180

We must begin with bloodletting.
If I ordered a medicine
At this point, as a physician
I would deserve much blame.

PATIENT: But bloodletting frightens me so,   185
And simply seeing my blood flow
Drenches my entire body
With cold sweat. I won't hear of it.

DOCTOR: You must show determination.
A grown man, endowed with reason,   190
And you behave like a young child
Frightened to death by foolish fear!

WIFE: Some have, and I have seen a few,
Been cured without bloodletting,
By drinking nothing but a brew   195
Made of the juice of red poppies.[18]

DOCTOR: Still your tongue, you silly woman!
All your chatter muddles my mind.
Until the Day of Reckoning
I'd see no end to your meddling.   200
I have never seen an illness,
No matter how hard the case,
Where some harebrained woman
Doesn't suggest cures by the score.
And if by chance but one is cured,   205
A multitude using that herb,
Unaware of its properties,
Will cause the death of the others.

(*He turns to the patient.*)

Well, then, the apothecary
Will supply what I have prescribed,   210
And you must do as directed
To recover soon and fully.

WIFE: Sir, we must tarry no longer,
Tell me what you wish me to order.
Do not budge from my husband's side: 215
Left alone, he might be afraid.

DOCTOR: You know neither gums nor grasses,
                And I will not give you their names.
WIFE: Indeed I have read the *Proverbs*
                And the *Voyages Overseas*.[19]   220
                You should not so quickly condemn
                Our receipts and remedies,
                But well you should admire them,
                For we hold them from the Boomans.[20]
                    Now, do write very slowly   225
                What you want my husband to do:
                He shall do it all faithfully,
                For he much values your wisdom.
                I shall not tire of listening,
                Do tell me what your pleasure is.   230
                And at this table, if you please,
                Put all this affair in writing.
MAIDSERVANT: Master, what does your heart tell you?
                What have men given you so far?
                And has the pain afflicting you   235
                Been subdued by this new doctor?
PATIENT: No, but I have become aware
                That one of the cures is patience,
                And that I soon relapsed in pain
                When I placed myself in man's care.   240
MAIDSERVANT: Now that you fully perceive
                Where the greatest good can be found,
                All false remedies you must leave,
                To remain with the true and sound.
                Faith alone will help you remain   245
                At all times healthy and happy.
                If you succeed in reaching it
                Among the contented you will be.
                    And when you can at last fathom
                That in God is your only life,   250
                This life you'll no longer cherish
                Or fear that it be snatched away.
                    You will not feel grief or longing
                For illness or even for health.
                Disease may torment your body,   255

But in that Life there is no death.
    And if your flesh is all you heed,
Torment and fear will never cease.
Death alone will give you the peace
That eluded you when you lived.   260
But serenity will be yours
When, alive, you are dead on earth,[21]
And peace will quiet all discord
In a new and gentle accord.
    And thus the soul, at last humbled,   265
And aware of its worthlessness,
Once it is from its shell unbound
(A body valued less than dung),
Suddenly sated with goodness,
It will be worthy to meet God,   270
So bound to its beloved bonds
That the Devil will have no hold.[22]
    At last, delivered from Evil
And from the torments of the flesh,
You will see your ills, born from sin,   275
Your vices, no longer concealed;
They will, with all their devices,
Burn in the flame of Charity.
Then you will know whether I lied,
For in truth you will be holy.[23]   280

PATIENT: Your argument bears no dissent,
And its truth I cannot deny.
I believe it and I feel content,
Free at last from my agony.
O God, who gave Your Only Son   285
To teach us the truth of Your Word,
Blessed are those who surrender
In submission to You alone!

DOCTOR: Here are my written directions.
I shan't return till tomorrow,   290
But give me my ducats now.[24]

WIFE: Here they are; hold out your hand.

PATIENT: Sir, under no circumstances
Shall I be bled. I can't bear it.

DOCTOR: Indeed you will.
PATIENT: Sir, I am fit.   295
         An illness can't last forever.
DOCTOR: I have never in my career
         Seen a pleuritic recover
         Without ample blood-letting.
         Are you no longer in pain?   300
PATIENT: No, Sir. But of solace I have
         Enough to sell, even to you.
DOCTOR: All this, my friend, is but fiction,
         And tomorrow we must bleed you.
PATIENT: Simply take my pulse, my good friend,   305
         And see my present condition.[25]
DOCTOR: Your fever is gone, I can see:
         Frankly, this is a mystery.
         You had one foot close to the grave
         From the pain, and for you I grieved.   310
         In this house I set but one foot
         And I find you hale and hearty.

         (*He angrily turns to the wife.*)

         Woman, tell me the truth: he took
         Some herb of yours, do not hide it.
WIFE: Truly, I am not about to speak,   315
         Seeing that you call me a fool.
DOCTOR: What have you done, tell me, my friend!
PATIENT: Not a thing that I could recall,
         But my suffering has ended,
         And what I have is my true faith.[26]   320
DOCTOR: Parbleu, it is a magic spell,
         An incantation or a charm.
PATIENT: 'Tis neither herbs nor amulets.[27]
         Words, more than witchcraft, have power.

         (*He turns to the maidservant.*)

DOCTOR: You, there, could what has just happened   325
         Be the fruit of your invention?

PATIENT: No, my friend, the words are so fine
That she needs no incantations. (*She laughs.*)

DOCTOR: Look at her, acting innocent,
While she mocks me behind my back! 330
She must have vowed him to a Saint:
Vowing to Saints is women's art.
Might not on her cheek a quick slap
Be exactly what she deserves?

MAIDSERVANT: Sir, the doctor is always praised[28] 335
When he heals, wouldn't you say?

DOCTOR: So you cured him, you low-bred wench,
With your spellbinding bewitchment?

MAIDSERVANT: That he is cured I am certain;
With what, and how, I don't know. 340

WIFE: Yes, cured he is, but do explain:
What remedy did you give him?

MAIDSERVANT: I gave him nothing but the Word,
As simply as God commanded.

WIFE: Do you mean the Pater Noster 345
Or Masses to be sung at dawn?[29]

MAIDSERVANT: But this receipt goes much farther,
For it can cure all afflictions.[30]

WIFE: What is it?

MAIDSERVANT: To trust the promise
Of The One who never deceives. 350

DOCTOR: But who has taught you such lofty thoughts
And this elegant gibberish?
It is the art of sorcerers
To confuse us with parables.
We have wise and learned doctors 355
Who have frequented colleges:
They are our only proctors;
To them alone we must listen.

MAIDSERVANT: But if what they say is nonsense,
Are women wrong to doubt their words? 360

DOCTOR: Listen to the way she answers!
Go fatten your geese in the field,
And see whether the hens have laid:
That is the place where you belong.

Fit to be tied or even hanged 365
Is what you are.

MAIDSERVANT: I am amazed
At your hatred of those who smile
To see my master in good health.

DOCTOR: The fire of Saint Anthony blast you!
Still I'm happier about this cure than you. 370

WIFE: Ignore, Sir, this pompous jackdaw.
But do tell me, for I must know,
Can a man, on his faith alone,
Be cured without remedies?

DOCTOR: Yes, I fully believe in signs 375
From God, and wondrous miracles.
And in the days of Christ divine,
All were healed without the arts.
But for now, the Holy Script
Tells us that we must show respect 380
For the doctor, and obey him.[31]
And Solomon, the noble king,
Who gave us from God the message,
To our honor paid homage.
God saw that his mortal creature 385
Could not be spared from illness,
And gave us the help of Nature
To free him from pain and distress.
These learned tomes we were given
By venerable physicians, 390
And a man would be besotted
To amend their ancient science.
The old remedies that you praise
Are good, and came from us doctors.
But alas, you haphazardly 395
Give them freely to one and all,
And what cures one may harm others.[32]
No brew of yours, sweet or bitter,
Should be dispensed, not even once,
Without a doctor's advice. 400
And you, the pretty maidservant,
Acting so pure and innocent,

	You cunningly seek to persuade
	That you heal with your oration;
	'Tis but a spell or a charade,
	Which may bring death to your master.
PATIENT:	Unless he sheds his lofty manner,
	He will remain in ignorance.[33]
DOCTOR:	My friend, if your illness recurs,
	Be blind to the truth no longer.
	Read the writing on this paper:
	It is your health, please understand.
	If you need me, I do intend
	To come at once, at your request.
	You pretend to have found your health,
	But the silver is mine to take.
PATIENT:	Little work he did for his gain,
	Returning to life the living!
WIFE:	But indeed he deserved his pay:
	He writes in a scholarly way.
PATIENT:	Dearest, this is but the chatter
	Of a too human opinion:
	With Faith I submit hereafter
	To the Greatest Good I am bound.
	This man wishes to be revered:
	His haughty pride is too obvious;
	He only speaks of laws and rules,
	And of the respect due his peers.
	But if we fill his hand with gold,
	He will often be in this house:
	Yet he would want us, I believe,
	To believe in him as in God.
	Out of danger I feel safe,
	By God's work, with no mediator;
	To Him alone, my only good,
	To Him forever, I belong.
	My determination will not fail,
	And thus I pray that all Christians
	May keep in Him, with whom I stay,
	A faith, like mine, everlasting.

NOTES TO *THE PATIENT AND THE CURE*

1. Censura in Librum sic Inscriptum: Epistolae & Evangelia ad usum Diocoesis Meldensis, November 6th, 1525.

2. She wrote four biblical plays: the *Comedy of the Nativity*, the *Comedy of the Adoration of the Three Kings*, the *Comedy of the Innocents*, and the *Comedy on the Desert*. All four were apparently performed in the castles of Pau or of Nérac by professional (Italian) actors hired by Marguerite, a detail revealed by an outraged Florimond de Raemond. Due to their length, we may assume that they were performed once on different days or at different Christmas seasons. All four were included in her *Marguerites de la Marguerite des Princesses*.

3. The monks, hidden behind the hedge, are an audience of which the devisants are aware, and we, the readers, looking over the monks' shoulders and obeying the author's beckoning, become the privileged spectators for whom she has written her book.

4. "Le Malade" as a title for this play reflects Marguerite's opinion that misguided faith is a disease that should be treated as such. In several plays, the characters speak of someone's "condition" when they refer to his or her attitude toward worship. Here, the man shows all the symptoms of an illness that the doctors cannot cure. It appears that the title "the patient and the cure" better translates the spirit of the play.

5. This physical thirst is of course a metaphor for his deep religious yearning, of which the audience is aware.

6. Saulnier suggests that the boar's tooth and other remedies offered by the woman represent a discreet allusion to the cult of relics in the Catholic Church, but one may wonder whether Marguerite would be so daring. She may simply point to the popularity of folk cultures among the uneducated.

    Line 24: She uses the word "cataplume" for "cataplasme" in the text. Because the word does exist in English as well, it seems logical to keep the malapropism.

7. She mispronounces the word *procureur*, (prosecutor) and is not too certain of what his function is in the community. She also makes the common error of attributing to his wife the feminine form of his title.

8. Raw eggs are still prized by many for their curative values, but Marguerite undoubtedly knew that five egg yolks would be excessive for a sick person.

9.   Lines 54-56: This stilted speech pattern is similar in the French text.

10.   Lines 61-62, 73-74: This is clearly an allusion to the then (and still) popular cult of most Saints in the calendar, which Marguerite would label a form of superstition.

11.   Once more, it is a simple person who enlightens the more affluent or better educated "sufferer": e.g., children in *The Inquisitor*, the chambermaid in this play, and with lesser success, Little and Less in *Most, Much, Little, Less* and the shepherdess in *Comedy of Mont de Marsan*.

12.   Matthew VII: 15.

13.   The author makes it quite obvious that in this perfect confession (which may possibly lead to the salvation that God has the sole power to grant) there is no intercessor. In other words, it is the absolute surrender of the patient to God, the "doctor."

14.   The well-meaning spouse eagerly (and thriftily) mentions remedies suggested by other women. The various concoctions mentioned by Marguerite were most certainly used in her day. Rabelais gives an extensive list of these folk remedies in the Prologue to his *Pantagruel*. If indeed the boar's tooth could be seen as an amulet, then these well-meaning but useless practices could be associated with the good works and superstitious rituals that Marguerite deplored.

15.   The French "Laissant aller au lard la chatte" could not be adequately translated in such a colorful manner: letting the cat eat the lard, i.e., letting what ails him kill him.

16.   Being awakened by this black-robed man touching his wrist, he is startled and briefly led to believe that the doctor is a priest who had come to give him the Last Rites.
Lines 165-66: It is ironic that his pain returns as soon as he deals with the world of men.

17.   Saulnier indicates that pumpkins are easily contaminated by elements in the soil in which they grow.

18.   When the plant or mineral used in the treatment was red, its therapeutic value for all blood disorders was considered certain. Rubies were worn for anaemia, and beet juice would undoubtedly be thought quite effective.

19.   She is understandably hurt when the doctor calls her an ignorant fool, and pointedly proves not only that she can read but also that she has read more than one book. "Les Proverbes communs" was a very popular volume in the sixteenth century. Cf. Brunet, *Manuel du*

Libraire, IV, col. 912-13. "Le Voyage et Itineraire de oultre-mer," by Brother Jean Thénaud, a Minorite Brother of Angoulême, is an undated volume, with a possible date of 1530.

20. Another amusing malapropism invented by Marguerite; here the woman, who has mispronounced a number of words, is alluding to "Bohemians." Marguerite clearly plays on the triple meaning of the word: natives of Bohemia; travelling gypsies; more obviously, the Bohemian Brethren, a sect formed from the remnants of the Hussites in the fifteenth century. They formally rejected the idea of transubstantiation, only admitted a mystical spiritual presence of Christ in the Eucharist, and took the Scriptures as their sole doctrinal guide. Most sixteenth-century reformers looked somewhat kindly upon them, at least in Marguerite's lifetime.

21. This rather ambiguous line reflects Marguerite's insistence that the Christian must be dead to the world of the living to contemplate eternal salvation.

22. The author uses the words "deslyée," "lyée," and "lyens" together to stress the bonding of the soul to God.

23. Lines 241-80: This long exalted argument may appear somewhat remarkable on the part of a maidservant, and her language is far more elaborate than that of the shepherdess in *Comedy of Mont de Marsan*, but the message is the same: she is enraptured by the love of God. For her, salvation is not in the hands of the clergy, but in the hands of The Only Doctor, God, if the "patient," the sinner, surrenders in absolute faith.

24. According to Cotgrave, coins "termed as duckets" were each worth 6 shillings and 8 pence. Saulnier indicates, however, that the ducats mentioned here were not gold, but (smaller) silver ducats worth 56 sols (each roughly the equivalent of $10 US?).

25. Now that he feels cured, he is far more casual with the doctor, whom he had treated with utmost respect earlier. The doctor had called him "my good friend" or "my good fellow" (mon compère) when he first addressed him. Now the tables are turned, and the patient calls the doctor "mon compère."

26. The author states once more that true and total conversion erases the process leading to it from the mind of the converted.

27. Because one meaning of the word "tourteaulx" was "small enameled figures," we have chosen "amulets" as a translation. Saulnier offered "flat, round cakes, thus an allusion to the Eucharist," but it seems doubtful that Marguerite would have dared such belittling of the

wafer.

28.   We must assume that the doctor did not carry out his threat, or that if he moved in her direction the maid slipped out of his reach. She does not appear to be overly concerned, and in her reply she speaks to him very calmly.

29.   The author stresses the simplicity of the wife and therefore of all those for whom worship consists exclusively of memorized prayer and impersonal rituals such as the mass. The maid will answer that the Word is far beyond this.

30.   For the French "recepte," the word "recipe" was tempting, but receipt, "something used as a cure or remedy," is far more logical.

31.   It appears that the doctor quotes the Scriptures to reaffirm his prestige and his own power. As Saulnier indicated, this quotation is from *Ecclesiastes* 38:1-3: "Honora medicum propter necessitatem; etenim illum creavit Altissimus. Disciplina Medici exultabit caput illius et in conspectu magnatorum collaudabitur."

32.   Lines 393-97: Saulnier stresses that this is a "double entendre," and that rather than dealing with the medical treatment of illnesses, this speech alludes to the fact that for one who is blind to the evangelical doctrine, reading the Scriptures should be left to the theologians who alone can and should comment on religious texts. In other words, they must memorize and repeat what has been taught by the "doctors."

33.   The patient himself, being totally converted, sees through the doctor's argument. The doctor had called most of the other characters "ignorant fools"; he is now condemned, for his excessive pride is seen as foolish ignorance.

THE INQUISITOR

(L'inquisiteur)

INTRODUCTION

Synopsis

A devious Inquisitor laments the fact that those who criticize his actions and who question those of the Church know the Scriptures better than he does. He then decides to go outdoors with his manservant, hoping to spy on a few unsuspecting victims. All he finds is a group of children happily playing in the snow, and he reproaches them for wasting their time instead of learning the teachings of his Church. To his dismay they laugh, which infuriates him, but they slowly defuse his rancor and his desire to harm them and their families. After hearing their simple and pure profession of faith and their song, the manservant and the Inquisitor are converted.

History and Comments

V.L. Saulnier convincingly suggests 1536 for the composition of this play, for which the chosen title of "farce" does not seem quite appropriate, because, like its predecessor (*The Patient and the Cure*), it is a modified form of morality play. The inclusion of a "Marot psalm" offers a tempting argument for a later date, but although his *Psalms* were not published until 1539, Marot had already translated several of them, among which the third (interpolated between lines 283 and 365 in this play) while he resided in Ferrara. It is a matter of record that when he was at last allowed to return from exile in 1536, Marot entered France at Lyons, the city where Marguerite spent most of that year, thereby joining his benefactress and his friends.

Scholars hate anonymity, and, from the *Chanson de Roland* to Proust's *Remembrance of Things Past*, volumes have been compiled in an effort to identify fictional or composite characters. The devisants of the *Heptameron*, who simply represented the feminine and masculine viewpoints associated with social rank, status, age, education and feelings, since they all knew one another very well, have consistently been provided with various names, titles and functions. As expected, the character of the Inquisitor has been given various identities: Etienne Mangon, Louis de Rochète, Jean de Roma, Noël Béda—all but the last dismissed by Saulnier. We might add to this list Bishop Erard de Grossoles, who formally accused Marguerite of protecting heretics, and who masterminded a bizarre plot to have her murdered as cleanly as possible by placing poisoned incense in the thurible that would be swung in her direction with pious vigor until the fumes surrounded her during Christmas mass. Béda, Marguerite's nemesis, might be a suitable model for the despicable character,[1] for in 1533 his religious zeal had carried him beyond the legal limits of his functions in his tireless pursuit of Roussel, whom Marguerite had invited to deliver the lenten sermons at the Louvre. This incident caused him to be promptly sent into exile,[2] and he certainly never saw the evangelical light. More than a composite of several unsavory characters in whose conversion Marguerite would have rejoiced, and in spite of this Inquisitor's total transformation at the end of the play, we see in him a caricature of evil incarnate, a disturbing presence mitigated by the compassionate hint that all sinners can be redeemed.

The manservant, on the other hand, is a realistically depicted opportunist who knows how to placate his master. No matter what he thinks, he remains respectful, fetches slippers and gloves, and speaks when spoken to. However, his transformation is very swift after he has watched the children, whose innocence he envies. Once he hears them speak, he feels the need to defend them and to join them. A simpler man than the Inquisitor, he will be converted sooner, becoming himself an instrument of salvation for his corrupt master.

Much has been written about the children's identity. Lefranc was of the opinion that they represented simple and honest people who spontaneously embraced the concept of an evangelical reformation as an expression of their true faith, and perhaps as well all potential victims of persecution. Saulnier rejects this thesis and suggests the following: Janot = Calvin; Clérot = Clément Marot; Thiénot = Dolet; Jacot = Lefèvre. One must admit that these nicknames evoke these men's given names. It has also been proposed that Thierrot is Luther, and that Pérot must be Bonaventure des Périers, because his translation of the *Canticle of Simeon* is the final song of the play; in the case of these two men, the phonetic similarity is more tenuous. Marguerite may indeed have wanted to intrigue her audience with such brain-teasers, because enigmas were fashionable and very popular, and two of her poems in the form of an enigma have so far remained unsolved. However, we agree with Saulnier, who (although he stood firm on his identifications) stated in his first edition of this work that one may reject every one of those hypotheses without denying that these "children" were purely and simply Marguerite's protégés.

These seven characters possess the innocence and the singleness of purpose of children, both in their games and in the faith that is the unquestioned staff of their lives. They are also remarkably witty and reveal a thorough knowledge of the Scriptures that is quite beyond their years. Finally, with the prudence of adults, they demonstrate the intellectual sophistication and the learned skill to deflect the Inquisitor's dangerous questions. While all possess child-like qualities, only one is a child; and it is he, significantly nameless—the one whose baby-talk reveals him to be the closest to perfect innocence—who will achieve the dramatic conversion of the Inquisitor.

The construction of this play is basically the same as that of *The Patient and the Cure*, but Marguerite has enriched the plot and added an effective element, that of veiled danger: the Inquisitor's soliloquy sets the mood, and the audience uneasily expects evil deeds to occur in the following scene. Had Molière borrowed this plot, he would have opened the play by placing on stage two or more characters speaking about the corrupt and cruel Inquisitor before that character appeared, thus making his dreaded—yet anxiously anticipated—entrance more dramatic, but there is no room in a farce for such theatrical devices. However, in this second farce Marguerite has refined her technique. She adds subtle allusions to various known authors, and she even seems to wink gently at her audience: those who had read Erasmus's *Herculei Labores* could hear an echo of his complaint about the ignorance of those who teach others. She also uses for the first time numerous comical elocution devices such as monosyllabic words and sounds that the children fully understand but that remain meaningless for the Inquisitor. Dialogues at two levels of communication, plays on words, puns, riddles—she spares none of the ambiguities and witticisms in which her privileged and well-informed audience must have delighted.

The persona of the Inquisitor is so evil in contrast to that of the children, and Marguerite has created in scene IV a mood so fraught with danger, that a juvenile or a less sophisticated audience (as is commonly seen at plays where a beast or a devious adult threatens an unsuspecting hero) would react spontaneously and shout warnings to the "victim." The tongue-in-cheek answers and the asides of the children lessen the man's oppressive aura by making him the unwitting object of laughter, but even a mature audience is keenly aware of the ominous danger and instinctively hopes that these innocents will be spared. And spared they will be, by their wit and by their mastery of the rhetoric of silence, a rhetoric that had become one of Marguerite's favorite devices, and of which we can find numerous examples not only in her plays but in others of her works.[3]

She also gives proof that she was somewhat familiar with the procedures of the Inquisition; the interrogation of the children is true to form inasmuch as it begins with a simple request for an identification of their parents, followed by simple questions inviting the desired answer, and then progresses from subtle cajoling to threats of violence.

As far as the children's games are concerned, Saulnier stresses that these were also played by Gargantua, which seems perfectly natural. Rabelais probably selected a few outdoor games that he knew to be popular with children and that, one should add, are still played today. Although we hear a clear echo of Thélème at least once in this work (lines 185-86), borrowing Gargantua's games would be quite unnecessary: Marguerite had undoubtedly seen many a child at play and knew their games.

We do not know whether this play was performed. Marginal stage directions such as those found in the manuscript of *The Patient and the Cure* could confirm that it was at least rehearsed, but none appear. In fact, all stage directions are clearly interpolated in the text, and this reveals a very important development: in the first play, stage directions were an afterthought, added during rehearsal when actors felt the need for guidance. In the second, Marguerite visualized these technical details as she was writing the play, and since her cast of actors was considerably larger, rehearsals—if the play was performed—must have been greatly facilitated.

That this play should have been omitted from *Marguerites de la Marguerite des Princesses* is easily understandable. Her hopes for a peaceful reform within the Roman Church had been shattered, her protégés were dead or exiled, and several had suffered a violent death (the latest being Dolet, who was burned at the stake in August 1546, the year of Luther's death). No reconciliation with Calvin was possible; the weakened evangelical movement was threatened; there was no middle ground and no dissent was allowed. Choosing between the Huguenots and Rome, a decision that she had certainly not contemplated in Lyons in 1536, had become for her a moot question. The decision was truly no longer her own in 1546, when she began editing her works for the 1547 printing, and *The Inquisitor* was not to be published. But if this comedy could not be seen in print, another, better, and far more subtle of her evangelical plays was waiting in the wings: *Most, Much, Little, Less.*

THE INQUISITOR

(L'inquisiteur)

The Inquisitor	*Children*: Janot
His Manservant	Pérot
	Thierrot
	Clérot
	Thiénot
	Jacot
	Small Child

SCENE I

INQUISITOR.

INQUISITOR: (*Alone.*) Times are getting forever worse;
Religion is of no account.
Our prestige, and this I much lament,
May too soon wane and bring us shame.
 This new knowledge eclipsing ours   5
Will rob us of honor and fame,
And thus I must, from the pulpit,
Speak each day till I destroy it.
 Were I only dealing with the ignorant,
I would frighten them back into the fold: 10
'Tis the scholars that I cannot silence,
For better than I they know Holy Writ.
No longer can I content them by feint:
Forever they seem to quote the Scriptures,
 Which I had truly never read with care, 15
And thus, much pain and toil I must endure.
 Learned theologians of the Sorbonne
Many years ago made me a doctor.

Four years now a Great Inquisitor
Of our faith, I have indeed spared none.   20
I shall not say that when I am offered
    For a man's life a substantial sum
    (But let not a word of this be whispered!)
    I am not promptly willing to save him.
    But a fool will allow himself to die: 25
    I can provide against him a witness,
    Yet he refuses to pay for his life,
    As reason and common sense would suggest.
    Although I see no reward in his death,
He will still burn in the fire of Hell,   30
But should he irritate my aching brain,
    I shall think nought of burning him alive.
    It is better that an innocent die
    Cruelly, as an example to all,
Than to see our sacred law decried   35
    By this persistent heretic fervor.
    If he dies innocent, gentle, and pure,
    The man is blessed: Heaven will be his!
But if he is evil, we may argue
That by making him die, we give him grace.   40
        Good or evil, it is clear and simple,
    All brought to me I commit to the fire.
    My only aim is to give examples,
And little do I care for the tortured.
    Many a man is somehow displeased   45
    With my rigor. I only scoff at them!
    My only wish is that because of me
    The means to torture be increased.
        If a friend or two, for my cruel ways,
Charitably attempt to reproach me,   50
    I never fail to say, "Alas, dear friends,
    'Tis but my zeal to chase from our land
    All those who might encourage the people
    To stray from the Holy Church and its Saints."
    I cleverly make what is black look white,   55
Because I cloak my wrath in piety.
        For all their complaints I care not a whit:

Sad or angry, it is the same to me.
I only look at my gain and profit,
And I assail those who uphold the faith.   60
Of good deeds I speak well, but what of it?
I do not care for the toil or the pain.
Faith has no appeal, and my creed is vague,
And I can relinquish my charge early.
    All I do rests on my deceptive mien.   65
I am a scoundrel and I play the pure:
Unless a weighty gift appeases me,
No creature alive ever has the wit
To escape me: I make him a pilgrim
On a long, distant, and painful journey,   70
Unless, wearing nought but a shirt, humbly,
He comes pleading for my pardon. Or else
He shall die by fire or rot in a cage.[4]
    But these thoughts have so excited my brain
That I feel the need (to lessen the pain)   75
To go outside; the weather is fine,
And I have not left the house for days.
So that I may better enjoy my walk,
Go fetch my shoes, and off with my slippers.
Against the cold I think it is healthy   80
To wear gloves: bring me my winter mittens.[5]

SCENE II

MANSERVANT, INQUISITOR.

MANSERVANT: Where do you wish to go, Master,[6]
In this ever-changing weather?
INQUISITOR: I can stay indoors no longer.
MANSERVANT: (*Aside.*) He has truly lost his wits: 85
—One cannot walk through this deep snow
That hides the path and the meadow.
INQUISITOR: I must worm out a secret
Or two from unsuspecting prey.

	Is it cold?	
MANSERVANT:	No, Sir, I think not.	90
INQUISITOR:	And how can you tell, varlet?	
MANSERVANT:	Because I see on the hillside	
	Children happily playing quoits.[7]	
INQUISITOR:	'Tis the reasoning of a dolt	
	When children play games in the snow,	95
	Build castles,[8] or run to and fro,	
	To conclude that it is not cold.	
MANSERVANT:	Master, I shall not take the blame.	
	Look at the children at their games:	
	They are all as rosy and warm	100
	As if they sat around the fire.	
	Either they do not know or feel	
	The very cold which gives you chills,	
	Or God protects little children	
	Better than you, old and sullen.	105
INQUISITOR:	(*Hitting him.*)	
	What fool is this? Will you be still?	
	Does it behoove you to say this?	
MANSERVANT:	You have truly hit me, Master!	
	I want to leave you forever.	
INQUISITOR:	Indeed you will not, for you share	110
	In the secrets of my affairs.	
MANSERVANT:	I am loyal, you must concur;	
	Then call me a fool no longer!	

SCENE III

Children: JANOT, PÉROT, JACOT, THIERROT, CLÉROT, THIÉNOT.

JANOT:	Pérot, 'tis your turn.[9]	
	I've thrown so close	115
	I'm near the goal.	
PÉROT:	You had set your aim	
	On this fair cypress:	
	You did win your claim.	

JANOT: Under its shadow,   120
                All troubles aside,
                Joyful and happy
                I shall rest quietly;[10]
                Its countless rewards
                Will surround me.   125
PÉROT: Janot, by my faith,
                You won before me
                And carried the prize.
JANOT: As you clearly see,
                Boasting is unwise: 130
                Chance was my teacher.

                (Two more children arrive.)

JACOT: Thierrot, let me fend
                And try to defend
                This fair castellet.[11]
THIERROT: I want to behold   135
                That with no delay
                It is mine as well.
JACOT: I shall defend it
                Until my last breath,
                With no fear of death.   140
THIERROT: I shall never cease
                To keep and hold it,
                There I long to be.

                (Two more children arrive.)

CLÉROT: Thiénot, come with us!
                We shall catch the bird   145
                That flies in highest.[12]
THIÉNOT: How fair it is!
                Plumage and body
                Worth more than a world.[13]
CLÉROT: I have one who soars   150
                And whose words surpass
                The great popinjay's.[14]

THIÉNOT: In his loving arms
                  Mine embraces me:
                  For it, words fail me.   155

SCENE IV

MANSERVANT, INQUISITOR
Children: JANOT, PÉROT, JACOT, THIERROT, CLÉROT, THIÉNOT.

MANSERVANT: But would you say, my dear Master,[15]
              That these little children are cold?
              It seems to me that where they are,
              Icicles warm them like a fire.
INQUISITOR: I would prefer that their parents   160
              Brought them to hear our lessons.
              Wasting their time in games and songs,
              Away from us they are misled!
              —Children, children, time is wanting!
              You would do better studying.   165
JANOT: If we are happy and content,
              Sir, you should not be so troubled.
INQUISITOR: What a frivolous contentment,
              To play with a castle of snow![16]
PÉROT: It is a fine recreation   170
              Where no evil is to be found.
INQUISITOR: You do nought—nay, you waste your time
              In things that benefit no one.
JACOT: If it does not bring perdition,
              A pastime should always be praised.   175
INQUISITOR: Children, it would be better still
              To know of good and of evil.
THIERROT: Of evil, to become wicked?
              (*Aside*.) He can truly try one's patience!
INQUISITOR: Wicked? This is not what I meant.   180
              It is to acquire virtue!
CLÉROT: Does one receive it in cubits,
              Or with a straw to measure it?

INQUISITOR:	Youth that is opinionated
	Never wants to learn what is good. 185
THIÉNOT:	Rabbi, the youth who are well-bred
	Know the lesson they need to hear.[17]
INQUISITOR:	Who taught these children to argue
	And to speak with such arrogance?
JACOT:	But who taught him to get tonsured, 190
	And to wear such fancy mittens?[18]
INQUISITOR:	Do you want to stay ignorant
	And waste away your youthful years?
PÉROT:	No, but we choose to rejoice
	In ever true pleasure and joy. 195
INQUISITOR:	What pleasure can you entertain
	From a game of such little worth?
JACOT:	But how can you see a game
	That has neither color nor form?
INQUISITOR:	I see the game in which you stray 200
	And wander far from doing good.
THIERROT:	Dear Sir, you tell us that you see![19]
	In good faith, I don't believe it.
INQUISITOR:	Don't I have two eyes in my head
	To see what is in front of me? 205
CLÉROT:	And so does, dear Sir, any beast
	That has no reason and no faith.
INQUISITOR:	This language is too harsh to bear!
	I need to know with no delay
	Who their fathers and mothers are, 210
	Or I would fail in my duty!
	My child, who is your father?
	With much care, describe him to me.
JACOT:	Yours!
INQUISITOR:	Not so! By God the Father,
	You and I are not related. 215
JACOT:	Since you refuse Him to be yours
	In spite of my telling you so,
	He is the Father that is ours
	Where one does not sing your praises.
INQUISITOR:	I have no need of his favors, 220
	Nor your parents' or your cousins'.

PÉROT: And He does well without you,
              Dear Sir, for He has good neighbors.
INQUISITOR: Who is he? Don't keep it secret!
              Tell me his name as well as yours.   225
JACOT: Dear Sir, to know Him, you must go
              To the priest who baptised Him.
INQUISITOR: How do you call him?
THIERROT: He comes
              To me always, and is not called;[20]
              But where he resides is so high,   230
              Sir, that you could never go nigh.[21]
INQUISITOR: I must know the house and the street:
              What sign hangs over the door?
CLÉROT: It is known of all the children,
              And you do not know where it is?   235
INQUISITOR: Is he a gentleman, a merchant?
              Or might he be a laborer?
THIÉNOT: In this way you will not find Him,
              For clearly you cannot know Him.
INQUISITOR: But is he father of all,   240
              Or does each of you have his own?
JANOT: He is Our Father, can't you see?
              We are the heirs of all He owns.
INQUISITOR: If he has money, he's a fool
              Not to send you to our school.   245
PÉROT: What we have and what we shall be
              We hold certain, and have no fear.
INQUISITOR: These are too clever repartees.
              I must know who instructed them.[22]
JACOT: Sir, I saw a bowl of cherries   250
              In which the reddest were taken.[23]
INQUISITOR: But if I take a switch to you,
              I shall make you tell me the truth.
THIERROT: We shall tell it if you insist,
              But you do not understand it.   255
INQUISITOR: I do not comprehend the truth
              When I am the one teaching it?
CLÉROT: Did you receive it for merit,
              Or for gain, like a good merchant?

INQUISITOR: Yes, indeed, I gained from it,   260
                And mine was a spiritual gain.
THIÉNOT: The preacher did his work too well,
                For he looks pure but is not so.
INQUISITOR: With my hand upon your arses,
                I must inflict your punishment.   265
JANOT: But, Sir, if your hand is not clean,
                You have no power to cleanse us!
INQUISITOR: These dangerous and foolish words
                Are not from the minds of children;
                They are, by God, much too brazen.   270
                I forbid you to speak further!
MANSERVANT: Master, you take too much umbrage
                At the words of innocent youth:
                You, who can subdue the famous,
                Must bear with trifles of that age.   275
INQUISITOR: Childhood or innocence, alas,
                I see nothing there but mischief,
                And shall not tire to strike them
                If they attempt to speak again.
MANSERVANT: Let us walk on, Sir, let them play: 280
                They speak no more for the moment.
INQUISITOR: What a good apostle you are!
                Have you taken their side?
MANSERVANT: Me? Nay!
CHILDREN: (*Singing.*)[24] O Lord, so many
                In their zeal to harm   285
                Bring us trouble and woe!
                O Lord, so many enemies
                Readying for battle
                Rise against us!
INQUISITOR: I hear them singing. What is this?   290
                It seems that they are mocking me.
MANSERVANT: They are children who, joyously,
                Sing as one voice in unison,
                As happy as birds in a tree.
CHILDREN: Indeed there are many   295
                Who say about me:
                "His strength is shattered. . .

MANSERVANT: They are far from melancholy!
CHILDREN: He no longer finds in his God
             Salvation anywhere. . ."   300
             But they are foolhardy.
MANSERVANT: Listen to their song, so joyful,
             You will be filled with happiness.
CHILDREN: For Thou art my unfailing
             Shield and protection   305
             And my true proven glory.
MANSERVANT: This is a good and timely song:
             I could not conceal its merit.
CHILDREN: It is Thou, truly,
             Who makes me march on   310
             With my head raised.
MANSERVANT: This brood has clearly not been hatched
             By evil birds.[25] Listen to them:
             With no discord, all united!
             I hear but one voice among them.   315
CHILDREN: I have lifted my voice
             To the Lord many a time,
             Speaking my complaint.
MANSERVANT: No cunning, no hypocrisy:
             Their hearts have not been perverted.   320
CHILDREN: He did not reject me,
             And from His holy mountain
             He heard my prayers.
MANSERVANT: Freely and without constraint,
             Playing, singing, ever joyful,   325
             Upon this earth never idle,
             But their eyes look up to heaven.
               If you grant me my leave, Master,
             Among them I shall remain:
             For I want to weep no longer,   330
             And I will share in their laughter.
CHILDREN: Thus I shall go to my sleep,
             And I shall safely rest,
             With no fear of being abandoned.
MANSERVANT: May God watch over them always!   335
CHILDREN: Then I shall awaken

	And without fear spend my days,	
	With my God as my keeper.	
MANSERVANT:	I think that all eagerly wait	
	For the time to dwell in Heaven.	340
CHILDREN:	One thousand men abreast	
	Will cause me no fear,	
	No matter what they may do.	
MANSERVANT:	Would to God that with no sermon	
	They would let me stay among them.[26]	345
CHILDREN:	And even if, to frighten me,	
	To surround and encircle me	
	From all sides they draw near me.[27]	
MANSERVANT:	And may their songs teach me so well	
	That, like them, I may live on faith.	350
CHILDREN:	Come to me, make yourself known	
	To me, my Lord, my King,	
	Who, with one blow, topples. . .	
MANSERVANT:	There is no deceit in their song. . .	
CHILDREN:	My snarling enemies,	355
	And shatters their teeth	
	In their devious mouths.	
MANSERVANT:	No quarrels, no controversy;	
	They have the Whole, nought is amiss.	
CHILDREN:	It is from Thou, God in highest,	360
	That we must expect	
	True salvation and protection.	
MANSERVANT:	How fortunate are children!	
CHILDREN:	To all people you confer	
	Always and at all times	365
	Your greatest blessings.	

SCENE V

MANSERVANT, INQUISITOR.

MANSERVANT:	I confess that felicity
	Is found only in innocence,

                  And in the light of their knowledge,

                  Learning, truly, is cecity.[28]   370

                  Verily, Master, they have reached

                  Total peace and understanding.

INQUISITOR: What do they know?

MANSERVANT: Everything!

                  With the exception of evil.

INQUISITOR: Their words are novel and subtle,   375

                  As handsome and young as they are.

MANSERVANT: Into an old wine-skin, Master,

                  One does not pour new wine, either.[29]

INQUISITOR: And who taught you of the Scriptures?

                  It is so written, to be sure!   380

MANSERVANT: 'Tis you who read the words to me;

                  But God gave me the spirit.[30]

INQUISITOR: Truly you make me think anew

                  Of what I never thought before.

MANSERVANT: Please do not scold them any more,   385

                  And you will then hear wondrous things.

SCENE VI

INQUISITOR, SMALL CHILD, MANSERVANT.
Children: JANOT, PÉROT, JACOT, THIERROT, CLÉROT, THIÉNOT.

INQUISITOR: Children, to you we return,

                  To hear your sweet songs.

CHILDREN: *(They put their fingers to their lips and refuse to answer.)* Uh-uhhh!

INQUISITOR: Alas, do speak to us!

                  Please overlook our scolding!   390

CHILDREN: Uh-uh-uh-uhhh!

INQUISITOR: Alas, my friends,

                  I was not aware of the words

                  That instilled such fear in you,

                  Indeed, I did not know you.

                  You, who are the youngest,   395

	Speak to me, have no fear.	
SMALL CHILD:	(*Baby talk*.) You are big and me little,	
	We could not reach you.	
INQUISITOR:	God forever true has said	
	That be it by toil or through pain	400
	Man will not gain the greatest good	
	Unless he be as an infant![31]	
MANSERVANT:	But even more, by a new birth	
	He who is not from above born again	
	Will never leap up to Heaven.	405
	I find this doctrine beautiful!	
INQUISITOR:	And I, having grown into an old man,	
	Might I truly be born anew?	
MANSERVANT:	No, Sir, there is no such remand,	
	But change you must, through and through.[32]	410
INQUISITOR:	How?	
MANSERVANT:	If you want to know the way,	
	Go to the children and ask them.	
INQUISITOR:	Children, enlighten me on this:	
	'Tis a request, not an order. . .	
CHILDREN:	Uh-Uhhhh. . .	415
MANSERVANT:	You hushed the boys into silence,	
	But if you question this infant	
	You will find there some mystery	
	To provide what you hunger for.	
INQUISITOR:	My child, what do you call God?	420
SMALL CHILD:	(*Baby talk*.) Dada!	
MANSERVANT:	'Tis very well answered.	
	Everywhere He is a father to all,	
	But He is seldom heard.	
INQUISITOR:	What do you hope to find in Him?	
SMALL CHILD:	Sleepy-bye!. . .	
MANSERVANT:	A fitting answer!	425
	For whoever knows only Him now	
	Lives at peace in tranquillity.	
INQUISITOR:	But, child, who is that God?	
SMALL CHILD:	Good, good!	
MANSERVANT:	No one could have said it better.	
	For so great is the gift of God	430

	That He cannot be called other	
	Than by the name: "The Only Good."	
INQUISITOR:	What of good deeds and of merit:	
	What is it worth?	
SMALL CHILD:	Tsah!	
MANSERVANT:	Oh, Lord, well said!	
	Our deeds are so small before God	435
	That they are worth less than nothing.[33]	
JANOT:	Since it is in good earnest	
	That you want to learn the truth,	
	You must listen and be patient;	
	It is our duty to speak.[34]	440
PÉROT:	To live in true contentment	
	There is but one point to be learnt,	
	And it is that to do good	
	Is not in man's power.	
JACOT:	By opening yourself to God,	445
	And letting Him do as He wills,	
	Your suffering will turn to joy	
	And you'll know yet-unknown bliss.	
THIERROT:	He who, losing himself in God,	
	Thinks not of himself nor of men,	450
	May be given of God the name;	
	By grace he is the Son of God.	
CLÉROT:	Alas, had Adam not eaten	
	Of the fruit of good and evil,	
	The Lord would not have punished him,	455
	Making him much worse than a beast.	
THIÉNOT:	He who, as did the Pharisee,	
	Contemplates himself or his deeds,	
	Will discover that he is bare,	
	And more unworthy than a cur.[35]	460
JANOT:	Whoever is dead to this world	
	Through the power of the Spirit	
	No longer lives but by his faith,	
	For in him lives Jesus the Lord.	
PÉROT:	Greatness, power, prestige, or worth	465
	Are of no concern for a youth:	
	God is both father and master,	

	The only way and only power.	
JACOT:	Leave Adam's self-important cares!	
	His body is an empty shell.[36]	470
	Separate yourself from the flesh:	
	True knowledge is beyond matter.	
INQUISITOR:	These children are speaking the truth:	
	I have read it in the Bible,	
	But the words they use, so simple,	475
	Reveal to me their true meaning.	
MANSERVANT:	Listen to what these children say:	
	Their sweet discourse is heavenly.	
INQUISITOR:	Happy is he who becomes a child.	
	This I want to be, more than wise.	480
MANSERVANT:	Master, I feel within my heart	
	Divine inspiration.	
INQUISITOR:	I feel that Christ the conqueror	
	Has cleansed me of all passions.	
MANSERVANT:	I no longer feel avarice,	485
	And my heart burns with charity.	
INQUISITOR:	Gone are my pride and my vices,	
	Smitten by the spirit of truth.	

          O powerful Spirit,
          O sweet Jesus,   490
          Who, by your mercy
          And your Holy Script
          Have destroyed
          My presumption,
          I am abashed.   495
               I think of nothing
          But pleasure and joy.
          I jump, I dance,
          And no longer know
          Who or what I was.   500
               My all and my path
          Are in God alone;
          I am less than nought.
          Fie upon ambition,
          Which is only sated   505
          With ordure and dung!

God, the only good,
And away from Him,
All is but torment;
I have and I hold   510
Of all Christians
The true fulfillment.
   Where is my sin?
I see it hidden
In the flesh of my King;   515
It is gone from me,
Who was soiled by it
And in disarray;
I can see clearly
With the eyes of faith   520
Salvation through grace;
I am dead, I know.
He who destroys evil,
My Christ lives in me.
   Sing, earth and heavens,   525
Your delightful songs
For this rare event:
From such an old man,
A vicious devil,
God made a young angel.   530
Let us so praise Him,
Who has suddenly
Metamorphosed him.
He seeks no revenge;
I go to His side   535
Ever so gently.

MANSERVANT: Divine providence,
             What story is this?
             Upon a persecutor
             Darkened by sins   540
             You had mercy
             Like a good shepherd.
             Of an Inquisitor,
             Inventor of torments
             By fire or by trial,   545

You were the victor,
And you made his heart
Gentle as a child's.
    I weep with joy,
Seeing at this hour   550
What I so desired.
And until his death,
If he remains so,
I shall stay with him.
God drew him to Himself,   555
Cleansed him from evil,
Of which he had much;
    As I sighed for him,
I shall now laugh,
Seeing him happy.   560
    O God, Way and Life,[37]
Thou who hast captured
His living soul,
Thou sated it so
That it yearns for nought,   565
And it is fulfilled.
With Thou it is one,
It is dead and lost
In mortification.
After defeating it   570
Thou hast received it
In exaltation.[38]
    As his manservant,
I tossed in my sleep,
Missed many a meal.   575
Seeing him with God,
I no longer regret
My toil and pacing.
    He's caught in the net
By the gentle lure   580
Of the Scriptures.
I shall never tire,
For better, for worse,
To serve him truly.

JANOT:	O eternal God,	585
	This day must by all	
	Be celebrated.	
	Of this cruel man	
	You have made a lamb	
	Similar to us.	590
PÉROT:	God catches wolves,	
	And without fail	
	Turns them into ewes,	
	For as the spouse	
	Of all, white, black, or brown,	595
	He is jealous.	
JACOT:	Far from forbidding us	
	To speak, he wants to learn	
	Our sweet message.	
	God gives good for evil,	600
	And always knows the way	
	To a man, at any age.	
THIERROT:	God with all His Heart	
	Loves what He has made,	
	And wants it perfect.	605
	And He is so wise	
	That we must let Him	
	Rule His own house.	
CLÉROT:	Well then, let us sing,	
	And with rejoicing	610
	Let us praise Him.	
	In towns or hamlets	
	Where we mortals meet,	
	It is remembered.	
THIÉNOT:	He will get a prize	615
	Who tells the story	
	To his companions:	
	Free from Purgatory	
	This man surely is.	
	There can be no doubt.	620
INQUISITOR:	My little ones, I beg of you,	
	For each of you to sing and shout	
	The glory of the God of men,	

               And let us together hold hands.

ALL: (*Singing together.*)[39] Since of your promise   625
               The accomplishment
               Bestows on my old age
               Perfect contentment,
               With no fear I shall wait
               For a merciful death.   630
                 As the last glimmer
               Of my fading eyes
               Has seen of your light
               The heavenly glow,
               I remain dazzled;   635
               My heart rejoices.
                 A light pure and clean
               You have sent to us
               So that our world
               Be cleansed from its sins;   640
               And its light so dim
               Shall glow clear and bright.
                 The light you provide
                 Will shine from afar
               For those who have strayed,   645
               Embracing the world,
               And your humbled people
               Will then nobly rise.

INQUISITOR: You have convinced me, my children,
               And thus with you I want to go.   650

JANOT: Won't you be treated with contempt
               For learning to speak as we do?

INQUISITOR: No, I deem it a great honor
               To follow you in word and in deed:
               And since it pleases our Lord,   655
               Innocently I want to live.

PÉROT: Come with us, and we shall lead you
               Within our abode of peace.[40]

JACOT: We shall never abandon you,
               And will sustain you in your task.   660

THIERROT: The two ladies of our house
               Are Unity, and Charity.

CLÉROT:	One eats there at all times	
	The bread of life and of truth.	
THIÉNOT:	Godspeed. May God, Our Father,	665
	Grant you good eve and good night;	
	May you always live in the light	
	Of the sun that forever shines.	
CLÉROT:	This is a most heavenly catch.	
	I haven't been happier this year.	670
	Let us have supper, the table is set.	
SMALL CHILD:	Let us go, let us go now.	

NOTES TO *THE INQUISITOR*

1. "Béda attacked humanists and evangelical reformers with the same vigor, not only in the name of the Faculty of Theology but *in the name of God Himself.*" (Cf. *Index des Livres Interdits*, Vol. I, *Index de l'Université de Paris*, p. 40.)

2. Cf. *op.cit.*, p. 46.

3. Cf. my article, "Silence as a Rhetorical Device in Marguerite de Navarre's *Théâtre Profane*," *Sixteenth Century Journal*, Volume XVII, Number 1, Spring 1986, pp. 17-31; but more particularly Robert Cottrell's splendid *The Grammar of Silence: A Reading of Marguerite de Navarre's Poetry*, Washington, 1986.

4. Following his escape from Ferrara via Venice, Marguerite's protégé Clément Marot was allowed to return from exile in late 1536. He agreed to be publicly scourged (wearing nothing but a shirt) in front of the Cathedral of St Jean in Lyons, the city where Marguerite resided most of that year.

5. He now addresses his manservant, who may have walked in (as a welcome visual break for the audience) during his lengthy monologue, and who probably stood behind him at a respectable distance.

    Line 81: When they were not used for Church-related ritual (in which case they were elaborately adorned), gloves were something of a luxury item. "Gants" may be used here as a general term, but

Cotgrave establishes a distinction between gants and mitaines, describing the latter as winter gloves. In other words, they were worn as a protection against the cold, while gloves added a touch of elegance.

6.   Scene I was written in decasyllabic lines; Scene II is entirely in octosyllabic lines.

7.   "Jouer au palet" was (and still is) a game in which each player aims flat, round stones at a specific goal. The word was later used for disks used in similar games (the puck in hockey, for example). It seems that "quoits" is a closely related game. Lines 132-33 and 135-36 seem to indicate that once a target was selected (castle, tree, etc.), the player whose "palet" was closest would claim it as his own.

8.   According to Littré, "châtelet" was a game in which children used walnuts or chestnuts to build small pyramids. In the context of the present work, it seems logical to assume that in addition to this "fortress" they are also building a small snow castle. Saulnier suggests that the children pelt a snow castle with nuts to demolish it, but this interpretation is totally inconsistent with lines 132-33 and 135-36.

9.   This scene is written entirely in pentasyllabic lines. This is rather formal speech for children, and they may be singing or quoting parts of hymns or psalms. For possible identification of these characters, see the Introduction to this play.

10.   The cypress is a familiar symbol of death, and the word "umbre" in the original is a play on the words "shadow," more commonly spelled "ombre," and "umbra." Janot alludes to the peace achieved with the death of the body and the divine protection felt by the true believer.

11.   Saulnier points to an important parallel: the castle being defended by the children evokes Luther's *Ein'feste Burg ist unser Gott*, of 1529. Translations of Luther's works were routinely dispatched to Marguerite, who copied or paraphrased many an excerpt in several of her works.

12.   The bird symbolizes the Holy Spirit or Grace.

13.   "Un monde," an allusion to the material world.

14.   A "papegault" was a parrot or a popinjay. Figuratively, "one thought to resemble a parrot because of excessive ornamentation in clothes, senseless volubility, or vain posturing." An allusion to Catholic decorum seems rather obvious here. Rabelais will later use the word "Papegault" to designate the Pope.

15.   The Inquisitor's and the manservant's dialogue is in octosyllabic lines; the children also speak in octosyllables but sing in pentasyllabic and hexasyllabic lines.

16.   It is with a certain reluctance that we accept Saulnier's choice of "snow" (based on Old French) for the word "noix" in this specific instance. Notes in preceding pages make it clear that the children play with walnuts as well as with snow.

17.   A "rabbi" is a master, a teacher versed in law. By using the name "rabbi" when they address the Inquisitor, they clearly depict him more as a lawyer or a prosecutor than as a Christian. Furthermore, he has already admitted that his victims know the Scriptures better than he, which makes him a poor or incompetent judge and teacher. Finally, his abrupt attempts "to teach the truth" are rejected by the children; Thiénot tells him that they already know the truth and that one does not "acquire" virtue. One senses once more a parallel with Rabelais's well-born and serene youth living at Thélème.

18.   Saulnier stresses that Marguerite, following Lefèvre d'Etaples (if he is "Jacot," this is significant), felt that numerous practices of the Church that were not found in the Gospel were unnecessary, if not laughable: the tonsure was one of those. Fasting and celibacy for the clergy were also listed among rituals for which no justification was found in the Scriptures. Needless to say, this is also in Rabelais.

      Line 191: Luxury in clerical garb and costly ornamented additions such as embroidered gloves were considered frivolous and ostentatious by most Evangelicals. The longer the cuff of the mittens, the more elaborate they usually were.

19.   Saulnier quotes the Evangelical dictum: "They have eyes and do not see, they have ears and do not hear." Cf. Psalm 115 of the (1560) Geneva Bible, "thei have eyes and se not."

20.   This is a clear echo of Lefèvre d'Etaples: one does not call God, He comes to the faithful.

21.   In the introduction to *Comedy On the Passing of the King*, Saulnier mentions one of Marguerite's letters to Briçonnet, in which she uses much of the terminology, including the image of the high mountain, also found in this play and in various poems.

22.   Lines 248-71: As the argument develops, the mood changes from laughter and amusing puns to an uneasy but prudent silence, and monosyllabic sounds or popular expressions that may appear nonsensical to the Inquisitor (but not to the audience). In *Most, Much, Little, Less*, the two peasants laugh, while in other plays shepherds sing

when pressed for an answer; since those who question them are adults, they consider the children dim-witted.

23. Pressed to give additional information, Jacot replies with a clever metaphor suggesting that he who says too much is soon singled out, precisely as the reddest and most visible cherries in a bowl will get picked out before the others.

24. Lines 284-366: This song, in which are interpolated octosyllabic comments or interruptions by the Inquisitor and the manservant, is the Third Psalm, *Domine, quam multiplicatsunt, qui tribulant me*, in Clément Marot's translation. We should add that these translations into French, which were instrumental in Marot's second exile, were repeatedly black-listed (in Marot's lifetime and after his death) by the Faculty of Theology of Paris. Cf. *Index de l'Université de Paris: Livres Interdits*. Centre d'Etudes de la Renaissance, University of Sherbrooke, pp. 421-25.

25. Lines 312-13: Old French proverb: "Vous ne fustes onques de mauvaise pie couvez": you are of no ill progeny, you have no taint of ill-progeny in you (cf. Cotgrave). In other words, these children are neither evil nor ill-bred.

   Lines 314-15: They are not divided into cliques, (a transparent allusion to religious discord among others).

26. A transparent allusion to sermons and lengthy glosses of the Scriptures, of which he is not fond, and which, he obviously feels, accomplish very little.

27. Lines 346-48 and 355-57 evoke wolves and ferocious beasts slowly encircling their prey. Georgette de Montenay's book of emblems gives several examples of lambs (adherents of the Reformed Church) pursued by the wolves of the Roman Church.

28. A familiar topos. Numerous religious emblems depict children playing happily, while scholars hold a lighted torch in bright sunlight that they cannot see or to which they are blind. Too preoccupied with words, they ignore the spirit of the Scriptures.

29. The manservant is converted in spirit: he quotes the Scriptures spontaneously to express his support of the children and their innocence (Matthew IX: 17 and Mark II: 22).

30. 2nd Cor. III: 6: "littera occidit, spiritus vivicat." Briçonnet also wrote to Marguerite that the true key to understanding the Scriptures was the spirit and not the letter.

31. Luke XVIII: 17.

32.   John III: 3, 4, 7.

33.   This sound and its interpretation by the manservant represent a very strong attack on good works and mechanical obedience to Church ritual. We find here a sentiment parallel to the criticism of the Ritualist in the *Comédie de Mont de Marsan.*

34.   Lines 436-71 represent a turning point: the children now speak clearly, and eloquently exhort the Inquisitor.

35.   Luke XVIII: 9-14.

36.   In this play as well as in several of her other works, Marguerite uses the name of Adam as a metaphor for our (worthless, corrupt, weak) body. Le "cuyder" represents conceit, presumption on our part. It is only when the truly faithful is dead to the physical world that he is alive.

37.   "I am the way, the truth and the life" (John XIV: 6). Saulnier notes that Marguerite was very fond of this quotation, which she used in numerous works.

38.   "Dilection" is the bond between souls founded on the love of God, a pious and tender love totally detached from the physical world.

39.   Lines 625-48 are Bonaventure des Périers's translation into French of *Simeon's Adoration and Prophecy* (Luke II: 29).

40.   The children are now the leaders; Pérot very openly and fearlessly invites the converted Inquisitor to join them in their Church, or at least to follow in their Evangelical footsteps.

COMEDY FOR FOUR WOMEN
(A COMEDY FOR TEN CHARACTERS)

(Comédie des quatre femmes)

INTRODUCTION

Synopsis

Four women, two of whom are quite young, blissfully happy and unmarried, the other two wretchedly unhappy in marriage, enter into a debate. An old woman, who has randomly and quite unexpectedly appeared, is asked to arbitrate, and she hears their stories. One holds her freedom so dear that she refuses to love; the second, loved and in love, claims that chaste love is true and everlasting; the third, who remains faithful although she has an adoring suitor, is very badly treated by her jealous husband; the fourth, who idolizes her husband, suffers because he loves another. They have not been given names and are simply designated as *first* and *second girl*, *first* and *second woman*, and *old woman*.

The old woman warns the first girl that whether she wants to or not, she will fall in love and suffer. To the second she says that love is fickle and happiness short-lived. She then gives the virtuous wife two choices: "Be patient: sooner or later your husband's love for you will abate and he will no longer be jealous; but, since he will mistreat you whether you are guilty or not, why don't you do and enjoy what you are falsely accused of doing?" To the unfortunate spouse, she says that an unfaithful husband is preferable to one who is not interested in sex, not to mention that "he can't come home contrite and pregnant!" If she is patient enough, he will tire of his new love, but taking a lover might make her feel better.

Needless to say, the two girls angrily reject the old one's pessimistic predictions, and the two disappointed women refuse her admittedly bizarre advice. As she is ready to leave, an old man engages her in conversation; four young men arrive, and all lead the five women in a dance in which the old man boasts that he may yet outlast the young.

History and Comments

This play, written around 1542, was called a "farce" in the manuscript, but a "comedy" in *Les Marguerites de la Marguerite des Princesses*. While the line between the two was blurred, the usually shorter farce was considered less noble than the comedy, and did not necessarily include a moral message. I found that distinctions between them were often tenuous and that the words farce and comedy were occasionally interchangeable, but—perhaps because of the deliberately comical dance that ends it—farce might better describe this unusual work.

In this debate on love, there is no plot. The sole attempts to proselytize are the testimonies of the two girls, which can only be meant for the audience, since they are of no value for the two women. The first girl declares that she finds in the love of God the strength to resist earthly love, while the second praises platonic love, but we are left with the uneasy feeling that, while both are blissfully happy at the time, their dreams—or at least those of the second girl—may be shattered. Furthermore, none of the characters will actually be transformed, or even remotely affected by the debate, which ends in a dance: their convictions and their situations will remain what they were when the curtain rose.

Ironically described as so majestic and impressive that the four others, awed, comment more than once on how respectable and dignified she looks, the old woman appears exhausted and near death, yet her spirit is very much alive. However, because she emphasizes the fact that she is one hundred years old and that she speaks an almost obsolete language, she clearly allegorizes the medieval tradition at its worst. Its ambiguous conventional values on love and marriage were still at the time the source of antagonism between Petrarchist authors and those who preferred popular farces and bawdy tales. Marguerite knew only too well, and deplored, the old woman's coarse yet very pragmatic mores, which her brother and her second husband gave her ample opportunities to witness, and which she grudgingly accepted. These ribald views on love, faithfulness, sex and marriage are precisely those of four of the men of the *Heptameron*, where Hircan and Saffredent promote the more casual and somewhat ribald attitude that the flesh is not to be denied, while Simontault, blasé, agrees with them to a extent, and Géburon, the eldest, warns the young women that men's intentions are seldom, if ever, honorable and altruistic.

Although clearly divided into two pairs, the four women represent four attitudes, four distinct views on love, which are also developed at length in the *Heptameron* and which, with the exception of Dagoucin's, are totally at odds with those of the men.

They also reflect on the one hand the beauty and the dangers of love, and on the other the unfair treatment of women in marriage, a situation that they are helpless to change as long as tradition nurtures it.

The first girl considers love nothing but the loss of freedom and the risk of suffering. Quite certain at the opening of the play that she can and will escape this dangerous passion, she offers no clues on how she will succeed. Lest we dismiss her as exhibiting the naive optimism and self-confidence of youth, we must note that it is she who speaks last at the end.[1] Her all-important final message (a finely crafted decasyllabic sonnet) stresses that our refuge is the love of God and that it is to Him that one must turn for the spiritual strength to resist earthly love. In view of the fact that she is young and unmarried, the possibility remains that she may later find a soul-mate and share the convictions of her opponent in this debate.

The second girl praises a mutual love that is purely spiritual. Detached from and surpassing earthly love, it is a union of two souls, a soaring in total freedom over the conquered flesh. This ethereal love, the most perfect form of friendship so praised by Plato, enthralled Marguerite, who discovered it in part through Ficino's *Commentaries on the Banquet*, translated into French for her at her request. It is seen in Dagoucin's idealized love for Parlamente, a devotion raucously mocked by Hircan and several of his companions in the *Heptameron*; we also find it lauded as a beautiful and desirable ideal more than as a reality in a few of Marguerite's poetic works.

The first woman is loved by a suitor who respects her honor and her wish to obey her marriage vows. She describes herself as honest and sincere, fearing God and jealous of her reputation. "Yet if her beauty is the reason why her husband loves her, why should not others also love her without her being condemned?" She does not flaunt her virtue, which would be committing the sin of pride, but her jealous husband insults and mistreats her to such an extent that she wishes for death. Of course, what is openly denounced here is a cultural tradition then—and perhaps still—accepted as natural by many husbands and lovers: on the one hand, the woman is bound to have invited the admiration and the adulation of other men and she is thus vicariously guilty; on the other, women had then very little choice if any in the matter of marriage and did not necessarily love their husbands. Whether she loved him or not, a woman remained the personal possession of her spouse, to be jealously guarded.

Logical as it may sound, the old woman's answer is somewhat cruel: "Time will solve your problem; when your beauty fades, he will no longer be jealous!" In other words, a woman is loved for her looks, and when she becomes less attractive, her husband will no longer love her, a pyrrhic victory at best. But, since thirty was considered the age at which women should be wise, since they were no longer beautiful, Marguerite's derisive rebuff of masculine values cannot go unnoticed. But the old woman also suggests an unexpected and more immediate means of consolation: "Have an affair with the man who loves you, because thinking of the one hour of pleasure you had with your lover will help you bear the remaining twenty-three with your husband." The offended woman reacts angrily and denounces such advice as vile.

The second woman is truly miserable because she loves a husband who loves another. She grieves when she is near him because he ignores her, and she suffers when he is away because jealousy devours her. The old woman tells her that she is really making too much of this: her efforts and all her tears will be in vain until his love for the other dims or until he becomes too old and ugly to be loved. She clearly thinks that it is man's nature to stray and that his mate must wait until his fancy passes, or, if he never reforms, until other women reject his advances. Marguerite's satirical intent is quite transparent, and she has more to say: the old woman adds that "she should be glad to see him interested in sex: many are not! Moreover, the appreciable advantage of roving husbands is that they can't get pregnant." Whether the distraught wife appreciates this homily is debatable, but the old woman finally analyzes her situation and provides a solution: her problem is that she loves him too much; he will come back to her in due time, and in the meantime she could find consolation in having a lover of her own.

At this point, Marguerite teasingly shows that the woman is, however briefly, tempted by this suggestion. We know that even as a form of revenge, Marguerite—whose husband had at least one mistress who bore him a son—did not condone infidelity on the part of a woman, and yet she makes it quite clear at this moment, perhaps as a warning to overconfident husbands, that some wives might follow such advice.

The messages to the women have been rather grim, and therefore the last two scenes of this play seem a very determined effort to make it entertaining. The appearance on stage first of an old man and then of four young men will create a transition and a total change of mood. In contrast to the four young men, the old man displays much courtesy, if not outrageous flattery, when he addresses the old woman, and one might hastily conclude that the older generation shows better manners than the new, but Marguerite only points to the enthusiasm and the lack of patience of youth. A parallel to the old woman, he is seen by the young men as "old, feeble and weak," but he is nevertheless vigorous enough to challenge them to a dance "in which he will outlast them." Indeed, he represents the other side of the coin in this allegory of the old medieval spirit, with his charming courtly manners, his sense of duty and service to the ladies; he is still perhaps capable of conquering some of the newer values, but he is also irrevocably bound by his age to the past, of which he and the old woman are the legacy.

When the old man gallantly commiserates with the old woman, she tells him dejectedly that the young women have refused her good advice, although what she had told them was "as true as the Mass." This interesting metaphorical choice is worth a pause: it would seem that if what was true in terms of mores for these two old people is no longer acceptable for Marguerite's generation, the Mass that was true for them might no longer be so either. In view of the fact that this play was performed before William Paget, British Ambassador to France, it is a clever joke that was bound to amuse Henri VIII, to whom Paget, in a letter of February 26th, 1542, reported having seen "this farce" at the French Court.

The old woman stays on center stage when the old man joins the four women in an attempt to convince them not only that her advice is sound, but that they are much in error if they do not follow it. Since he has not heard the debate, he is either nobly defending the old woman, or blindly bound to the tradition she represents, when he engages them in a dialogue that cannot be heard.

At this point the four young men arrive or come out of hiding. Watching the entire scene, they observe the old man, wonder about his intentions, and decide that he is lecturing them or preaching to the women, a thought that appears to irritate them. One suggests pushing him or beating him to chase him away, but his three companions indignantly refuse; another has a better idea, which is that if the four of them invite the four women to dance, the old one will no longer bother them with his advice. This solution may be as altruistic as it may look and they may have sought all along a way to meet the four women, only to see their plan foiled when they find them conversing with the old man. Not so easily dismissed, the old one challenges them: they will change their tune when he and his old companion outdance them.

No stage directions are included in the text, but the action is obvious and somewhat limited for a 745-line play. The length of several of the monologues, the fact that all five women are on stage for over 600 lines, and the basic absence of a plot leading to a denouement, may have lessened the entertaining impact of this play, and we must assume that its success was due to the energy and the enthusiasm of the five young court ladies who played the principal roles.[2] It is only with the addition of the last two very brief scenes introducing the five male characters that a light-hearted and animated ending could be justified, and the amusing dance was probably most appreciated by the audience.

This comedy represents a timely departure from Marguerite's usual dedication to religious writings. Analyzing various facets of love, she defends "pure" love from the attacks of those who mock the spiritual exaltation achieved when the temptation of the flesh is conquered. She lauds total devotion, faithfulness and self-abnegation for the two souls united in total freedom from earthly torments. Longing for gentler, more refined mores, she offers this moderate and peaceful contribution to the raging "Querelle des Femmes" pitting the Petrarchists and neo-Platonists against those who support the bawdy and earthy tradition that "Venus is to be obeyed." However, attacks from the "anti-pétrarquistes" had done more than ridicule spiritual love: they also offended the dignity of virtuous women, whose sincerity was questioned, if not denied. A piqued Marguerite thus turns the table, and, under the guise of "motherly" advice from the amoral old woman, she denounces the self-indulgence of masculine vanity. She then gives as examples two sincere women who, in spite of the suffering caused by the actions of their philandering or unfairly suspicious husbands, and an invitation to retaliate, choose to remain faithful.

The five attitudes on love represented in this comedy by the five principal characters can all be found in the *Heptameron* on which she was working at the time. The keen reader can already hear sotto-voce the voices of Parlamente, Ennasuitte, Longarine, Nomerfide, and the gentle Dagoucin. However, in the *Heptameron*, Marguerite will wisely divide into four diverse masculine voices the earthy old woman's odd counterpoint to the female chorus.

Nearly twenty-five years ago I rashly suggested that the end of each tale of the *Heptameron* opened the curtain on a mini-comedy that we, the readers turned spectators, were privileged to watch, over the shoulders of the monks sitting behind the hedge. Having compared the devisants' conversations to one-act plays, it seems as clear now as it was then that some of the characters in her *Theater* were the embryo of future devisants, and, paradoxically, that her comedies were a rehearsal for the stage of the *Heptameron*. If Marguerite's ten devisants are such believable fictional characters that scholars still attempt to give them "real" or "authentic" identities, it is because she had already seen and heard them in plays such as this one, when she made them her story-tellers. Interestingly enough, V.L. Saulnier indicates that he had originally called this untitled play "A Comedy for Ten Characters," but that he arbitrarily changed the title to "A Comedy for Four Women," which he found more appropriate. It would seem that his original title underlines better the literary importance of this play.

COMEDY FOR FOUR WOMEN

(A Comedy for Ten Characters)[3]

Two Girls   Two Married Women
An Old Woman   An Old Man
Four Men

SCENE I

FIRST GIRL, SECOND GIRL.

FIRST GIRL: All the pleasure and the satisfaction
That a sincere and gallant heart may find
Is the freedom of body and of mind
That gratifies every man, bird, or beast.
Wretched is he who, for gift or request,   5
Binds himself in such servitude.
I, for myself, have so charted my course
That my body and my heart will be free.
No one could ever by solicitude
Wrest away from me this worthy resolve.   10
SECOND GIRL: How foolish are they, and empty-headed,
Those who have professed that a virtuous love
Is for a heart prison and servitude,
And that love means a lady's misery.
Their false advice will not make me afraid   15
To fall in love, knowing that all that's good
When compared to Love is of no value.
He who has Love enclosed within his heart
Will think of his bond as freedom,
And could have no other desire.   20
FIRST GIRL: I would rather forever hold my tongue
Than claim that it is better for a heart
To be vanquished than to be the victor

          Over this love that you so highly praise.
SECOND GIRL: Is it conquered? But that makes it stronger.   25
          For a lone heart, loveless, is but ice.
          Love is fire, giving radiance and grace,
          Life, virtue, but for which the heart is nought.
FIRST GIRL: Freedom is the only suitable way
          To banish from the heart all fear and shame.   30
          As for me, I cannot possibly think
          Of anything that could wrest it out
          From my own heart.
SECOND GIRL: I do not wish to try
          To deprive you of a virtue so dear;
          But true Love must also, I do insist,   35
          Be called freedom.
FIRST GIRL: Thus, to conclude:
          You do maintain that Pleasure and Passion
          Are one, and this I cannot comprehend.
          But I have learned quite well that in Freedom
          One may find the source of every pleasure.   40
SECOND GIRL: But it is Love that kindles pleasure anew,
          For whenever I can hold close to me
          The one I love, no evil can touch me,
          And the many ills that fell upon me
          Seem to disappear from my memory.   45
          In this Love and in this goodly pleasure,
          Freedom itself is what allows a choice.

SCENE II

FIRST WOMAN, SECOND WOMAN.

FIRST WOMAN: It does much harm to a decent woman
          Who fears her God and prizes her honor,
          When her husband, with a too-wicked tongue,   50
          Wants to ignore the goodness of her heart.
          If my beauty deserves that I have a suitor
          By whom I am honored as well as loved,

Must I thus be less worthy of esteem
When my heart remains unblemished by sin?   55
Nay! but I should rather be reproved,
If not to sin were, for me, worse than sin.[4]
SECOND WOMAN: For a true Love, a reciprocal Love
Is the acme of its greatest desire.
But if one Love spurning the other Love   60
Chooses another Love, far less worthy,
It is a sorrow that knows no reprieve,
Time, or repose, to seek consolation.
Desperation is worse than death,
And jealousy is true desperation.   65
O broken Faith and too obvious offense,
That from you, worse than death, I must receive!
FIRST WOMAN: And so you think, my sister, that you have
The worst of ills, which you call jealousy.
Yet it is nothing but a fantasy   70
Compared to the cross that I have to bear.
Morning, noon and night I wish I were dead,
For my husband mistreats me so badly,
And for no reason, which vexes me more:
He is much to blame.
SECOND WOMAN: So, your body hurts: 75
'Tis a gentle pain, since it's not within.
Your only suffering is to listen.
But if you had to endure in your heart
The bitter pill that is mine to swallow,
Then you would own that if I sigh and weep   80
I have a good reason.
FIRST WOMAN: Reason, you say?
When from morning to night, and endlessly,
I am reviled, accused and chided more
Than a vile adulteress caught in the act?
For me, alas, such an honest woman,   85
To be so called! Ah, I could not be one!
It breaks my heart.[5]
SECOND WOMAN: Mine is breaking as well,
For this love that wages an endless war
Condemns me, unloved as I am, to cherish him.

He loves another, and I can't bear it. 90

SCENE III

FIRST GIRL, SECOND GIRL, FIRST WOMAN, SECOND WOMAN.

FIRST GIRL: What might these two women be discussing?
SECOND GIRL: And what makes them be so melancholy?
FIRST WOMAN: What reasons have these girls for rejoicing?
SECOND WOMAN: They very much appear to be happy.
FIRST WOMAN: Let us discover the cause of their glee. 95
SECOND WOMAN: I would like to.
FIRST WOMAN: Girls, God be with you,
    And may His loving smile be upon you.
FIRST GIRL: Ladies, may He also watch over you.
    You seem overwrought by melancholy.
SECOND WOMAN: We want to know if it is of folly 100
    Or of virtue that you so gaily speak.
SECOND GIRL: But seeing you weeping and moaning so,
    We wondered if our pleasure is greater
    Than the grief by which your hearts are saddened.

SCENE IV

OLD WOMAN, FIRST WOMAN, SECOND WOMAN,
FIRST GIRL, SECOND GIRL.

OLD WOMAN: Time, ever doing and undoing its work, 105
    Has been my teacher for one hundred years.
    Its great treasure, that it reveals to few,
    Was shown to me, and I have learned it well.
    For twenty years, I loved freedom so dear,
    Never consenting to have a suitor. 110
    Twenty years thence, I submitted to love.
    But he for whom I lived, and he for me,

    Was taken from me, much against my will,
    And for sixty years I have mourned my fate.
FIRST WOMAN: Here is indeed an authentic Lady. 115
    What a garment! What a face! Such bearing!
SECOND WOMAN: Alas, my friend, how ancient she is!
FIRST GIRL: This is truly an authentic Lady!
SECOND GIRL: One hundred years provide much experience.
    Oh, and how wise she could claim to be! 120
FIRST WOMAN: Here is indeed an authentic Lady.
    What a garment! What a face! Such bearing![6]
SECOND WOMAN: Let us go forth to her and approach her;
    We can only become better for it.
FIRST GIRL: In good earnest, I am very eager 125
    To listen to her well-advised discourse.
SECOND GIRL: But look at such a pleasant countenance:
    Let us greet her and bid her a good day.
FIRST WOMAN: May the Almighty in Heaven above,
    He who has sole authority on earth, 130
    Confer upon you all prosperity.
OLD WOMAN: My daughters, may He who has the power
    Fill your hearts, and may He enlighten you
    To know Him and your own selves as well.
    But who or what brought you unto this place? 135
    Do not keep it secret, I beg of you.
SECOND WOMAN: The desire to hear you speak,
    And thus to learn much good from you,
    But also to bring to your ears
    A question on which we argue. 140
OLD WOMAN: Alas, so many years weigh upon me,
    I am afraid that my ancient language
    Is no longer part of common usage,
    And that you will hardly understand it.[7]
FIRST GIRL: Please, madam, be not too weary, 145
    And listen to our debate.
SECOND GIRL: And we fondly hope to rejoice,
    Hearing your venerable words.
OLD WOMAN: If you expect cheer and solace,
    Each of you must in turn promise 150
    To tell me and present her case,

So that I may give my advice.
Be as swift as the sun above,
For my aged catarrhic head
Distrusts the cool vesperal haze.   155
Aware of my experience,
I shall say in good conscience
To each of you without praise
What to do and what lies ahead.

THE FOUR: *(Together.)* Among us four, who will be first?   160
OLD WOMAN: With no arguing, the wisest.[8]
FIRST WOMAN: I am the one!
SECOND WOMAN: And so am I!
FIRST GIRL: Gramercy, indeed, my ladies,
            If you are wise and we are fools!
SECOND GIRL: Their claim to be wise is in words,   165
             But we are so by our deeds.
OLD WOMAN: To bring this debate to an end,
             You, the first among those married,
             Explain to me why you are afflicted.
FIRST WOMAN: I have a spouse unworthy of my love: 170
             Yet I love him as much as God commands.
             On the other hand, an esteemed suitor
             Seeks me always and begs for my favors.
             My reputation, so dear to my heart,
             Demands that my virtue be respected,   175
             But my spouse makes me pay the punishment
             When I have neither sinned nor even erred.
             In front of all I speak to my suitor,
             Whose only wish is to obey and please
             So discreetly that save for a liar,   180
             No one can accuse me of wrongdoing.
             This irksome man forces me to be still,
             Alas, when I would rather be speaking,
             And to please him, to turn my eyes away,
             With much regret, from a more pleasant sight.   185
             For if he sees me speak, very angry,
             Before all he behaves so strangely
             That I must in the beloved presence
             Change from a pleasant to an angry talk.

It is a sorrow gnawing at my heart.   190
But when I attempt to avoid such grief,
And apply myself to what he wishes,
To dissuade him from excessive anger,
Doing nothing that might irritate him,
He then embarks upon a mad raving,   195
Swearing to God and inviting Devils,
And accuses me of always lying.
But it would be madness or mockery
To try to appease him with kindness.
He knows no peace until I am aggrieved   200
And my repose increases his furor.
A thousand names, to worsen my grief,
He calls me, the least of which is "wicked."
Alas, there is no reason or pretext,
For I am quite innocent of this vice.   205
That is the song that night and day he sings.
I bear it all, yet have nothing to gain.
But my virtue and my reputation,
In which I delight, cause me endless pain.
I shall always be an honest woman: 210
He does not think so and does me much wrong.
But I cannot find a single manner
To be comforted or to give solace
To my lover, who loves me very much;
I fear for my good name and my conscience.   215
Losing my mind, my senses, my patience,
Helpless, I can't endure and wish for death.

SECOND WOMAN: If it pleases you to hear of my woe,
Which had its source and was born in my heart,
You will not possibly entertain doubts   220
As to the fact that you have never heard
Of a greater one. For I have possessed
The greatest bliss to which I could aspire.
But then, the slow, dulling power of time
Turned this happiness into misery.   225
For more perfect a man could not be found
On the face of the earth than my husband.
And I believed him to be mine alone:

Alas, I see that my mind is straying.
He loves elsewhere: there is my death, my war.   230
I cannot tolerate it, or bear it.
I pray to God that a swift thunderbolt
Would take away his ladylove or me.
I see nothing that could give me solace.
I look everywhere, but fear seeing him,   235
Because when I see him I cannot bear
That in earnest, truly, he loves elsewhere.
And for a while I forced upon myself
To suffer it, hiding my emotions,
Thinking that life is made of many days,   240
And love is found in many forms and shades.
My good intentions were to no avail;
I have lost him, and he has a mistress,
Who has taken possession of his heart.
He leaves me his body, that is true.   245
His body with no heart adds to my misery.
The closer he is, the less joy I feel.
But far from him, my heart is in distress,
For I desire to see him constantly.
Be he near or far I know only grief.   250
And the worst is that my love increases,
So that I no longer know which to choose:
Seeing or not seeing, each torments me.
All night long, unable to sleep, I wail,
And I regret the unacknowledged love   255
I have for him, from which his new lover
Takes all the joy that was mine in the past.
I burn, I am on fire; I am cold, I sweat;
I'm in a fever: but the sole doctor
Who could make me whole takes my life away.   260
And at this point I shall end my complaint.

FIRST GIRL: Virtuous liberty[9]
I guard readily
With no distraction.
For love and folly   265
From melancholy
Cannot be parted.

When I heard talking,
Coming and going,
These foolish lovers,   270
I end up laughing,
And I tell myself
That they are wretched.
    Away with affection:
Away with passion   275
That can break one's heart.
My heart is my own;
My faith is not meant
To be given or sold.
    Whatever I see   280
Fills my heart with glee
And with true pleasure.
If one pesters me
I soon despatch him
For my peace of mind.   285
    I love my repose:
I flee the discourse
Of love and his band.
Whoever should plead
For my love would reap   290
Nought but his demand.
    I love verity;
I love purity
Of heart and body.
Affection and love   295
Find there no abode;
I cast them away.
    The jealous amuse me;
The surly anger me.
I live as I please.   300
Of dejected Love
Pleading for mercy
I deny the grace.
    I mock all of them
And I want no man   305
To be my suitor.

For their emotion,
Hate or compassion,
Do not touch my heart.
Their hidden secrets,   310
Their wretched regrets,
I hear very well.
As to my spirit,
I am so discreet
That they learn nothing.   315
    I am quite eager
To do a favor
To who deserves it.
And my compassion
Can change into joy   320
Their desolation.
    But pride I bring down,
And I leave alone
All would-be lovers.
If they weep or beg,   325
The louder they cry
And the more I sing.
    Thus I have no care,
Not even one (Thank God),
To rob me of sleep.   330
Whoever loves vice,
Folly, or deceit,
Pays too dear a price!
    I shall remain free,
Not taking the risk   335
Of falling in love.
Let love who so wants;
We shall in the end
Turn away from them.
SECOND GIRL: A virtuous love   340
    (Not at all sinful)
    I want to defend;
    'Tis no less seemly
    Than fair and pleasant,
    As one must keep it.   345

When Love becomes bound
To a heart still clean
Of all wickedness,
It gives it grace,
The words and daring   350
To be accepted.
    Without love, a man
Is very much like
A lifeless image.
Without love, woman   355
Is sullen, odious,
Unpleasant, and foolish.
    For Love, in tourneys,
Armors are fastened,
Lances are tilted,   360
Horses are spurred,
High leaps must be jumped,
And dances performed.
    He who doesn't love
Is foul and dirty,   365
And badly attired.
From good excluded,
His worth is no more
Than that of a straw.
    I love and am loved,   370
Esteemed and valued
By one, good and wise,
That I want to love.
I vowed to do so
My entire life.   375
    I think of him always,
And only feel whole
Or well when I see him.
Far from him I sigh,[10]
And in tears and cries   380
Do more than my due.
    When I see him again,
He sits by my side,
And hearing his words

I have such pleasure   385
That I do not wish
To go to Heaven.
    My heart is not mine:
It beats with his own.
But in this exchange   390
I find much delight;
All my ills vanish
In one brief instant.
    What happens to me,
Torment or menace,   395
I take in good part.
Love makes my heart fly;
It is the good school
Where I learn all good.
    I would not dream of   400
A stroll, even one step,
Not thinking of him.
He is for my ills,
My pain, my travails,
Refuge and support.   405
    He who thinks of love
As a jail, a dungeon,
Is much in error.
Love is, I believe,
The source of blessings,   410
And this until death.
    For the servitude,
The care, and the pains
Of love mean to me
Joy and liberty,   415
As long as I see
My sweet friend always.
OLD WOMAN: Daughters, all this disagreement
I have often heard debated.
Such quarrels are not new to me.   420
There are others, many more and
Greater cases to be argued.
Among those, some came before me,

And I, familiar with the root
Of these cases, knew very well   425
Which cure to order for them.
And thus to you I will provide,
I hope, profitable advice.
       You whose grief is unbearable
From a jealous and irksome spouse,   430
I beg of you to be patient,
For time will bring the help you seek.
It will deliver his heart
From the love of her whose beauty
Is the source of his cruelty,   435
Unless he is a foolish dunce,
With no sense, no brain, and no head,
To make him listen to reason.
Or else, if perhaps your patience
Can no longer bear with this dunce,   440
Make of him a most pleasant bird,[11]
For if you cannot make him fly,
He is of no comfort to you.
Whiling away the time you weep,
At least you will have one hour   445
That will help you bear, while he sings,
The twenty-three others.
Indeed this too-distrustful grouch
Richly deserves this song to sing.
Do not think of killing yourself.   450
Apply yourself to do your best,
Hoping to bring him to reason,
But he must be totally changed.
If he is changed, and you as well,
Your troubles will come to an end.   455
There is but one source of solace,
And it is this transformation.
FIRST WOMAN: Madam, I prefer to suffer,
And to bid for torment and death,
In spite of his maliciousness,   460
Than to do such a dastardly deed.
OLD WOMAN: Very well, time will see to it.

And when he sees you, quite ugly,
Since he so prizes your beauty,
He will leave you, much to your shame.   465
For, frankly, I have never seen
A disgruntled man be redeemed.
SECOND WOMAN: And I, forsaken by my spouse,
Won't hear advice to be followed?
OLD WOMAN: Yes, really, it makes good sense.[12]   470
You want to put out a fire
Before night; it would be better
To let it burn than see it cold.
If your husband, full of fire,
Loves another sincerely,   475
It is proof that he is not dead.
While he does you a little wrong
By sojourning elsewhere too long,
At least he can return to you,
And does not ill-treat you for it.   480
Would you prefer him very ill,
Lying down inert all day long?
And his eyes to all pleasures closed,
Unable to enjoy beauty?
Let him do what he has to do,   485
Since he does not belittle you.
Fear not this unending fever,
For, with time, it will grow weaker.[13]
And at least, though he is straying,
He can't come home heavy with child.   490
Do what he does. It's tit for tat.
Loyalty is what troubles you.
He is a lover, be one too.
When he loves no other but you,
You will love no one but your spouse.   495
You must follow his example.
Your love is a little too strong,
And his is not equal to yours.
It is for a Jewess or a pagan
To be such a slave to her spouse.[14]   500
Nothing will cure your lunacy

But to love him in the manner
That he loves you, or you will die.
For little, little or more. For nought, nought.[15]
And if you do not win this game,   505
You will do nothing but torment
Your heart and soul, and tear your limbs.
Time, from which you hope far better,
Will make him so ugly and old
That he will no longer please you.   510
You will wish that you could again
Become jealous, and he smitten.
But you will far sooner meet death
Than you could return to your youth.
And yet, whether love or old age   515
Were to bring an end to your grief,
The most acute will be deceived.

SECOND WOMAN: You give me very little hope
After too long a suffering,
Promising either a torment   520
Or a ready panacea
That my conscience could not accept.

OLD WOMAN: Therefore you must no longer moan,
For I have said what could be done.

FIRST GIRL: Madam, it is now my turn.   525
Happy I am and want to stay.
What does the future hold for me?

OLD WOMAN: What will it be? Alas, dear one,
I see that you are not aware
Of the immense power of time.   530
Hear ye! Many have I seen glad
That they could not have wished for more!
But quite abruptly from cloud nine
I have seen them tumbling down low.
I esteem and laud your delight.   535
Virtue, in making you perfect,
Has thus given you happiness.
But do not give it such quarter
That you look down upon others.
Love is a skillful false angel   540

Who cruelly takes his revenge
Upon those who made light of him.
For whoever has pride fears shame.
The more he sees you, good and fair,
Boasting of your cruel disdain,   545
The more he strives for his arrow
To strike your heart and make it his.
From this so far he has refrained,
Having found no one so perfect
As to be worthy of your love.   550
But if only once your soul-mate[16]
Is placed by Love before your eyes,
You will love as no one ever
Has loved; of this I am certain,
For it is Divine Providence   555
That in due time will see to it.
Until then your heart will be free
From love: you are too sensible,
I can see it in your bearing,
And you do not lay idle claims.   560
Love, who goes on stealing hearts,
And time, who silently passes,
Though your spirit is unyielding,
Will make, in spite of your resolve,
Your heart flutter, your pulse quicken,   565
And you will taste the bittersweet
That one has to endure for love.
FIRST GIRL: I deny it and shall stay firm.
Never shall I be teary-eyed
And suffer any emotions   570
Of love or of affection.
OLD WOMAN: Through ignorance you do not see
The value of my prophecy.
But whenever it does occur,
The Old One you will remember.   575
SECOND GIRL: I fear, madam, and want to know
Whether time may have the power
To put my great love in danger.
OLD WOMAN: My lass, for you I feel pity,

In that your great felicity   580
Cannot indeed last very long.
The heart of man is so fickle
And time is so very fleeting,
Opportunities that arise,
All the words that come and go,   585
Confirm Love as a fickle creature,
Whatever he vows and attests.[17]
Alas, my lass, he lied to me.
He presented me a suitor
In the spring of my tender youth   590
Such that with no goddess above
Would I have wished to change places.
My sweetheart I loved more than God,
And I thought that he loved me too,
With which no one could disagree.   595
But see what Time has done to me:
My suitor, so very perfect,
He took from me with no respite,
From which I have suffered such spite
That sixty years after, I mourn him still.   600
Old I am, but I often long
For the happiness I have lost.
Now you know of the misery
That in my heart will always be.
You will not fare any better,   605
For Time, who today presents you
With a gift of pleasure and joy,
Much as he has within your heart
Slowly fanned the fire of love,
Will gradually dim its ardor.   610
Thus you will suffer such anguish
In your spirit and in your flesh
That from within, your soul may leap,
Unless it is halted by God.
Alas, you are fated, I see,   615
To experience as much torment
Because of love, as contentment.
SECOND GIRL: Lo, Old One, whoever believed you

Would languish in pain and sorrow.
But the ocean will sooner rise   620
And the firmament roll downward
Than such a fate will befall me.
I believe none of this fancy.
OLD WOMAN: My lass, you cannot escape it,
And will say, much against your will,   625
"Alas, the old woman told me!"
SECOND GIRL: Lo! May my heart be by God accursed
If I believe in your discourse!
FIRST GIRL: Neither do I, being no dolt.
All she brings forth is misfortune.   630
OLD WOMAN: Aha! You will have a suitor,
And he will make you change your tune.
FIRST GIRL: I would rather go raving mad.
Without love my heart will be,
Free it will live, free it will die.   635
And I thumb my nose at lovers.[18]
FIRST WOMAN: My fearful heart, full of desire,
Knows not what advice to follow,
To love another or to wait
For time to pass, as she predicts.   640
But I would deem it foolhardy
To refuse a pleasure so near,
And wait longer for another.
OLD WOMAN: Take the time to think, if you will,
For you must never close the door   645
On opportunity when she knocks.
If you don't seize her by the hair,
She flies away with violence,
Leaving nothing but repentance.
Think wisely in this affair.   650
FIRST GIRL: Indeed I shall without fail.
SECOND WOMAN: My brain, my heart, my memory,
Are dismayed. I must not believe
In this prophesying sibyl,
For the more my mind endeavors   655
To hope that time will do its work,
As she says, the less I think it will.

For the far too great love I feel
For my husband will make me die
Rather than take another love,   660
And will prevent me from living
Until the time of sad repose
She promises, which gives me grief
Greater than I have ever felt.
OLD WOMAN: You will know no peace until then.   665
One might imagine such a dream
That would not at all be untrue.
The good Doctor did speak of it.[19]
Truly you cannot escape it,
All four of you, willy-nilly.   670
But, dreading the consequences
Of the night air, I shall retire.
FIRST WOMAN: What, you will leave us lamenting,
And tell us nothing worth hearing?
OLD WOMAN: Well, bring your struggle to an end: 675
This burden is mine no longer.
I pray that God, the King of Peace,
May sate your brains with his wisdom.
SECOND WOMAN: She is returning to her house;
We cannot make her stay longer.   680
FIRST GIRL: But what caused her to come hither
In order to tell me a lie?
That I shall love, 'tis mockery.
Love in my heart will never be.
SECOND GIRL: That my love will abandon me?   685
This deceiving old woman lied.
For never shall we be parted,
I from his heart and he from mine.
FIRST WOMAN: To break this virtuous bond of mine
Or to become foul and hideous   690
As this odious woman told me,
Truly her words will become lies.
Seeing me worthy of his trust,
My husband will believe in me.
SECOND WOMAN: May the Great Fire set her ablaze,   695
Wanting me to love, or to wait

Until old age or want of strength
Reform my husband. But I hope
That due to my perseverance
He will promptly return to me.   700
Then all my cares will disappear.
FIRST GIRL: The great sorrow and urgency they felt
Caused them to look to creatures for comfort.[20]
Our nature, filled with curiosity,
Made us want to know what the future held.   705
The time, her years, the knowledge and the skill
Of this seemingly judicious Lady
Made you reveal of your heart the secrets,
From which nothing but evil we could gain.
From this entire discourse we conclude   710
That to know the future is the domain
Of Him who holds true power over us.
To Him we pray and implore, as we must,
For as King of this earth he makes you see
That only in Heaven must your reward be.   715

SCENE V

OLD MAN, OLD WOMAN.

OLD MAN: Where are you going, kind Lady?
And where are you taking your youth?
OLD WOMAN: In all fairness, my gentle friend,
Upon a bed for want of strength.
OLD MAN: I see there many in their youth.   720
Were you with them?
OLD WOMAN: Yes, I just left.
I spoke to them true as the Mass,
But what? They do not believe me.
OLD MAN: I shall speak to them so clearly
That they will, I think, understand.   725
OLD WOMAN: Their brains would have to be mended,
For I told them all.

OLD MAN: I understand.
            But confirming your own discourse,
            I shall tell them even more.
OLD WOMAN: I shall wait, to see if his words   730
            Are received better than my own.
OLD MAN: Ladies, unless I am deceived,
            You are very much in error
            If this Lady you don't believe.

SCENE VI

FIRST MAN, SECOND MAN, THIRD MAN, FOURTH MAN,
OLD MAN.

FIRST MAN: What could this old man want with ladies?   735
            How frail and feeble he is!
SECOND MAN: He wants, I think, to save their souls
            Without our challenging him.
THIRD MAN: Our hearts shall not be so wanting
            As to push or beat an old man.   740
FOURTH MAN: Let us lead all four in a dance,
            And you will see them well taunted.[21]
OLD MAN: Taunted, no: but we challenge you,
            My Old One and I, to the dance.
            So, with no more thoughts, let us dance;
            You will see them swallow their pride.[22]

NOTES TO *COMEDY FOR FOUR WOMEN*

1. With the exception of a brief dialogue between the two elderly characters and a few remarks by the four young men who appear in the partly digressive scenes V and VI, which are not part of the debate itself.

2. Marguerite, future duchess of Berry, and Marguerite's niece; Marguerite de Bourbon, duchess of Nevers; Jacqueline de Long vic (Mme de Montpensier); Louise de Clermont-Tallard (Mme du Bellay); and the duchess of Etampes, favorite of the king. I find it difficult, for reasons of court diplomacy if not of simple courtesy, to accept R. Lebégue's suggestion that Mme d'Etampes, eldest of the ladies *and the king's mistress*, played the part of the amoral Old Woman. It seems more likely that one of the young women played this part with gusto.

3. Saulnier indicates that the manuscript bears no title but that of "farce" for this play. The 1547 edition simply calls it "comédie." His subtitle, "A Comedy for ten characters," seems far more appropriate than the accepted title. I have suggested in my doctoral dissertation (*L"Heptaméron: Contribution à l'étude de la pensée politique et sociale de Marguerite de Navarre*, University of Texas at Austin, 1969) and more particularly in my book, *Les Devisants de l'Heptaméron, dix personnages en quête d'audience*, a clear parallel between the characters in Marguerite's theater and those in the *Heptaméron*. We need not stress that the five women narrators also represent three generations, and that their views on love are quite similar to those found in this play.

4. Saulnier reads line 57, "Si je faisais de non pécher péché," as "if this harmless flirtation became an affair." I think that this is not an accurate reading, and suggest that, in this woman's opinion, her husband would only have the right to condemn her if not succumbing to her suitor's ardor were for her a pain worse than the remorse of sin. The fact that she has no desire to be unfaithful to the husband she loves absolves her from all guilt.

5. The ambiguity of the French text is respected, as it reflects the woman's anger and her dismay. "I am not one of those" refers to "adulteress," and not to "honest woman."

6. Lines 121-22 oddly duplicate lines 115-16 spoken by the same character. Marguerite may have wished to stress the young woman's awe, but we cannot dismiss the possibility of a lapsus.

7.   Madame Oisille makes a nearly identical statement before narrating the seventieth tale in the *Heptaméron*, that of the Châtelaine de Vergy, to stress the fact that because of her age she speaks an archaic language. Needless to say, it is a ploy to stress the authenticity of this very old tale.

8.   The old woman shows a keen knowledge of human nature when she requests no arguing among the women as to who will speak first: she knows that all four will claim to be the wisest.

9.   Lines 262 to 417 are stanzas of six pentasyllabic lines spoken by the girls. Saulnier indicates that lines 270-74 are the theme of a popular song. It would seem that lines 262-417 were sung rather than spoken. A study of the melodies used by Marguerite in her *Chansons Spirituelles* might be in order, but too few have been found to warrant a search for the original lyrics.

10.   "J'escritz" is often misread as "I write," but it is an apparent misspelling from the verb "escrier" rather than the more common "escrire" (to write).

11.   The word "coucou" (cuckoo) is not mentioned, but the old one's message is clear: the woman should make a cuckold of her husband. He will not learn how to fly, but when he "sings" his insults twenty-three hours a day, she will at least have the consolation of knowing that she enjoyed one hour at his expense.

12.   This line should be read as sarcasm on the part of the old woman: you want to kill a fire rather than let it die of its own, as that of the fireplace does at night. Wait until his passion for his lover wanes, and he will come back to you.

13.   Although the old woman is clearly alluding to another type of fever, she first mentions "la continue"; Saulnier indicates that is an ongoing fever. Cotgrave describes it as "a continuall fever whose fit never ceaseth till the disease, or diseased, end." Then she refers to "la quarte," quartan fever, a less persistent and dangerous illness, which afflicts the patient every fourth day. The straying husband's yearning for his mistress will grow weak, until he stops seeing her altogether.

14.   The allusion to the submission of all women in the Old Testament and in the Koran seems to be the only example in Marguerite's works of a woman advising another, as a Christian, to commit adultery as a form of revenge for her husband's unfaithfulness; this advice will be rejected.

15.   These charming alliterations, "ou peu, peu ou prou; ou point, point," defy translation.

16.   As indicated by Saulnier, "vostre moytie" here means "the person who is meant for you," and "soul-mate" seems to best reflect the intensity of this neo-Platonic metaphor.

17.   In the French text, "Amour" is capitalized whether it suggests the emotions of love or a personified Eros. In this translation, the word is only capitalized when it represents an allegorical character involved in the action.

18.   *Le Grand Larousse Encyclopédique* describes "faire la figue" as an obscene mocking gesture in which the tip of the thumb is shown between the index and the middle finger. For want of an appropriate translation, one may choose "I stick my tongue out to them" or Saulnier's "je leur fais un pied de nez," which seems more fitting.

19.   The good Doctor is God.

20.   Read: to seek comfort from humans rather than from God.

21.   The fourth man makes a play on the words "danser" and "tencer," because the young men assume that the old one is scolding the women.

22.   Saulnier logically notes that young persons of the queen's entourage most likely played the part of the old couple, and that indeed they could make a point of outdancing those playing the other characters.

MOST, MUCH, LITTLE, LESS

(Trop, Prou, Peu, Moins)

INTRODUCTION

Synopsis

In their opening soliloquies, two wealthy and powerful men tease the audience with enigmas, ostensibly to reveal who they are. They weave a complex net of riddles that prevents the audience from fully identifying them, but one may deduce that one represents the corrupt element of the Roman Church or the Papacy, and the other a temporal ruler. Both have donkey's ears, and all their efforts to conceal these appendages under elaborate head-coverings are fruitless, which greatly saddens them. Their path crosses that of a peasant and a shepherd, who appear to be blissfully happy if not enraptured by the sheep's horns that pierce through their hats. The two paupers cannot avoid being engaged in conversation by the two others, of whom they are afraid, but charitably attempt to end the vexing problem of their obnoxious ears. Most and Much agree to submit to their remedy, but finding the cure too painful, they resume their travels, while Little and Less follow their own path.

History and Comments

Most, Much, Little, Less, a far more complex work than the three comedies that we have read so far, reveals an evolution in the author's skills as a playwright, not only in terms of dialogue, but more particularly at the visual level of stage presence. Indeed, in spite of the fact that they had personalities of their own, all characters in plays such as *The Patient and the Cure, The Inquisitor*, and the *Comedy for Four Women* were anonymous beings solely identified by their occupation, their social status, or their physical condition: inquisitor, manservant, patient, old man, spouse, chambermaid, woman, or girl. This identification explained or justified their attitude and their behavior: "the man" as head of the household; wives and servants of either gender as devoted but thinking subordinates; "women" would be either married or older than "girls," who still think of love and dream of happiness. In this religious satire, written late in 1544 or during the early months of 1545, not only does Marguerite choose not to indicate the occupations of her four characters, leaving them tantalizingly vague, but she gives to each of the characters a name that is, euphonically and psychologically, the perfect reflection of his personality, names of which Cratylus would no doubt approve. Trop and Prou (Most and Much), mono-syllabic words in which the harsh "r" follows a consonant, are strong, forcefully projected, rounded sounds: those who bear those names are bold, powerful, and rich men. Peu and Moins (Little and Less), on the other hand, subdued and weaker sounds—one a closed syllable, the other a nasal softened by the initial "m", almost a whisper—do not strike the ear: they suggest the meeker and far gentler characters of two humble men of no account on the social scale, one who owns little and the other even less.

Although who or what they are remains deliberately clouded, it is undeniable that the four characters represent two ways of life and two incompatible philosophies; one may therefore wonder why we see and hear four men rather than two. Marguerite was aware that a lengthy dialogue between two antagonists of unequal social rank was unrealistic: each would feel threatened and thus reveal very little about himself. She knew as well that since she needed to conceal her clues amidst trivia, a revealing monologue such as the Inquisitor's would reach an awkward and tiresome length. The problem was logically solved with "inside-dialogues," that is to say, conversations with a confidant, far more acceptable to an audience than unrealistic monologues. The dialogues between each set of characters provide the audience with numerous clues as well as with much tongue-in-cheek humor before the four men engage in conversation. The unexpected "discovery" of a soul-brother will enthrall Most and Much to the extent that they almost feel giddy with relief and garrulously embark on a highly comical crescendo of revelations of their minor and major flaws, of their evil deeds, and even of their egocentric if not megalomaniac aspirations.

Marguerite wisely and successfully avoided the pitfall of stereotyping by infusing subtle differences in the personalities of Most and Much, one slightly subservient, seeking to please the other and agreeing with him at all times, and in those of Little and Less, one being far more fearful and cautious than the other. In fact, while Most and Much appear to be mirror-images of one another, they are true complements of one another, hence their delight when they meet: each feeds the other's ego as well as his own with praises and flattery. On the one hand, Most and an evil character of another comedy, the Inquisitor, have much in common, including their calculated indifference to torture for innocent dissidents (such as Evangelicals). Both share the heady thrill of religious repression. I agree with Petit de Julleville's thesis (rejected by V.L. Saulnier) that Most represents most abuses of the Roman Church: gold, lace, embroidery, frills, elaborate and superficial decorations, to cover weaknesses or sins, indulgence for one's greed, cruelty, venality, and thirst for total power.

As for Much, Petit de Julleville believes (and I with him) that he is a secular ruler, and Charles V seems a likely "victim" in view of the obvious pun on "Ostrich/Austrian" eggs and several hints at constant wars and territorial ambitions, not to mention his need of Rome to enhance his political and popular strength. Both characters represent the powerful in love with power, the wealthy eager to acquire more, those who are envious, corrupt, cruel, keenly conscious of evil but totally unrepentant. These characters, intelligent and well educated but devious men, have never experienced poverty, hunger, or oppression. They are blissfully vain, insensitive toward the humble, obsessed with the mundane, and particularly terrified of death. They take great pride in their physical appearance and in the elegance of their attire, which is a mask or a façade, but are unaware that they have lost sight of the spiritual element in their lives. Their sole preoccupation is to protect their dignity by hiding their large and pesky donkey's ears, an embarrassment that they share, and that is for them indeed a great source of distress. Every material possession is theirs, and their temporal power is such that it can remain unchallenged, yet Marguerite's lesson is that their "all" (le Tout) is in fact "nought" (le Rien). They are fools in Marguerite's eyes because they refuse the painful road to redemption that would impose upon them humility, austerity, and charity, all leading to the ultimate Truth that the other two characters have found.

Little and Less are poor, humble, amazingly serene, and happy. Less, obviously the poorer of the two, is more fearful, more cautious in his dealings with the powerful than is Little. They are seen as fools because they sing and laugh, unabashedly delighted with the horns that pierce through their hats, appendages of which most men would be ashamed. In fact, flaunting all "good sense," they revere these horns, which they consider the source of their happiness and of all consolation during their harsh lives. Unlike

Most and Much, they do not complement one another: they are equally sincere, honest, innocent, and kind, and they have no need of psychological reinforcement. They are "whole," and their uncomplicated companionship is founded on affinity, shared hardship, compassion, Christian love. Peasants or shepherds, these humble and joyful keepers of the flock clearly represent the Evangelical pilgrims for whom the temporal is worthless and for whom man is nothing until he finds God. This temporal "nought," their "rien," has led them to the ultimate Truth, the most desired "All" (le Tout). And thus the much-admired and respected Most and Much are the fools, while the two horned fools are truly the wise. Saulnier suggests that Little and Less are those harassed or pursued by the Faculty of Theology of Paris and more or less successfully protected by Marguerite: Pocque, Quintin, Rabelais, Bonaventure des Périers, but specifically Dolet, who—in spite of her efforts—was to be burned at the stake in 1546, and this thesis cannot be disproved. It seems quite possible that they are simply the anonymous mass of Christians who wished for austerity and humility within the Roman Church, those who had been swayed by the Cénacle of Meaux, those who valued the Scriptures over dogma, those finally who yearned for faith, pure and simple.

There has been much speculation about the symbolism of the ears and the horns in this play. Should the ears simply be seen as indicating stupidity or folly? Are they to remind us of Midas, who had the gift of turning everything into gold but who unwittingly made the wrong choice between two gods? Saulnier suggests that they indicate a spy, but he also stresses that in religious iconography the donkey symbolizes those who are not chosen, which is why in nativity scenes we see it at the left of Jesus while the (chosen) ox is on the right side. I feel that the comical evocation of "Midas!" whose name is called four times in one line on two different occasions, followed by a no less hilarious "Alas, alas, alas, alas!" leaves little room for doubt.

With regard to the horns, Marguerite states clearly that they are neither flesh nor bone, yet they not only repel but even harm all who attack them. As a symbol of true faith, they cause intense pain when inserted in the ears of the two corrupt and unrepenting characters. Saulnier reminds us that horns have been, from antiquity, a symbol of sovereignty, of which he gives a few examples.

One should add that they can designate the chosen one: Moses, the only character of the Old Testament to whom Christ expressly likened himself,[1] is often represented with small horns. Furthermore, horns are seen in the Scriptures as a symbol of aspiration toward the ideal of love, wisdom and redemption: "The God of my rock, in Him will I trust; my shield, and the horn of my salvation, my high tower and my refuge; my saviour, thou savest me from violence."[2] It cannot be altogether coincidental that Little and Less specifically speak of their horns as their refuge and their protection from violence as well as the instrument of their salvation. Their efforts to help Most and Much fail because those two characters have not found God, whose Grace alone could grant them the salvation that cannot come from men. Little and Less's God is glowing and warm, like the Sun ("notre Soleil"), and if for Most and Much God is dark and vengeful, it is simply because they are blind to His light, and in spite of their long ears they are deaf to His word. They think of Death as ominously black and violent, while for Little and Less it is translucent and serene.

One may wonder whether this sharp satire only received its *imprimatur*—when far more benign works were blacklisted—because it was listed as a farce among the "serious" works of the *Marguerites de la Marguerite des Princesses*. It seems more likely that it was not condemned because it included no *obvious* mention of the Clergy and made no *direct* reference to the Scriptures in ways that could be read as straying from established dogma. Marguerite's deliberate ambiguities as to the possible identity of her characters (we have already noted that she had mastered the rhetoric of silence) may have lulled the censors of the Parliament into the casual reading of a satirical farce involving insignificant shepherds and selfish men. These scholarly gentlemen were obsessed with transgressions of the Roman tradition, criticism of the Roman ritual, and forbidden translations into French of the Scriptures, but they do not appear to have been exceedingly witty, and the least one may say is that their sense of humor had long breathed its last.

This play is indeed a satire. It condemns pride, the pursuit of glory, the love of material goods and earthly pleasures, and more particularly violence and the abuse of power. However, its proselytizing message, far from flattering for the Roman Church, is clear: Marguerite sadly concedes that Rome has won over Meaux and its disciples, and that it will remain all-powerful. Flawed as Most and Much may be, they will doggedly pursue their Midas-like lifestyle, acquiring more riches, crushing those enemies who were or are still foolish enough not to yield to their warnings or their threats. Blind and deaf to the divine message of humility, charity, and compassion, they will console themselves for their incurable sadness by adorning their bodies with extravagant garments and their abodes with golden idols, and they will create monuments to their own glory.

Toward the end of their conversation with Little and Less, Most and Much begin to realize that they have revealed far too much of their nature to these paupers, a familiarity that they now regret, and one senses a dangerous note of resentment and of repressed anger when they abruptly decide to leave. Little and Less, having cautiously abandoned their efforts to help them hear the ultimate Truth, will however not follow them. At the end it is Little and Less, the meek, who invite the allegorized Roman Church and the powerful Emperor to pray for the dead, no doubt those who died for them or because of them: "The resurrection is not for all: many are called but few are chosen." Little and Less leave together, serene in their religious contemplation. Most and Much are gone, their roads have crossed, the dialogue has ended, nothing was accomplished, life goes on, the "farce" is over.

MOST, MUCH, LITTLE, LESS

(Trop, Prou, Peu, Moins)

Most   Much
Little   Less

SCENE I

MOST.

MOST: May he who must know who I am[3]
Descend to the depth of the Pit,
Speak to those who sing louder,
To those who roam from door to door,
And those who, watching passers-by,   5
Shoot them with unseen sarbacanes;
Those whose every word is a lie,
Those to whom all things are given,
And those who gleefully lament
Their gain, that another has lost.[4]   10
  My name is soft and lovable,
So needed, so agreeable,
It can be said by one and all.
My surname is awe-inspiring,
But yet no less admirable   15
Than one that no one dared to read
At the time of the wrath of God.
It is not unlike the Spirit
Whose name was, and is, the fairest
Ever written into a Book.   20
  My dominion and my office,
My condition and my functions,
Are mightier than is this Earth:
No fish could, but for the crayfish,
Reach it. For this jurisdiction   25

Is mine and cannot be conquered.
My role is to create thunder,
Yet I am a wicked coward.
Waging war in the name of peace,
I weave the noose and tie the leash.   30
    I have such a splendid abode
That next to it that of the Lord
Seems a dingy hospital ward.
My pastime and only pleasure
Is to play with fire and water: 35
In those is my recreation.[5]
On gilded wood, on solid stone,
I am seated: there I repose.
But alas, the year is too short
To do all that tell I dare not.   40
    I hide beneath this cloak of mine,
So tightly spun, so wide and fine,
That when caught, no fool can escape.[6]
My coat is of newly-shorn wool,
And I have enough caps and hoods   45
To make another man a cape.
With my gloves I catch one and all,
And once held in my hand's firm grip
None unscathed can ever escape,
Because I so swore and promised.[7]   50
    But you, who think yourselves so wise:
Unless you are as dull as calves,
You may perchance know who I am;
My bearing is ever harmless;
Be it weekdays or holy days,   55
Your eye could see no better man.
My power, so vast and mighty,
Exceeds human understanding.
I am he, to speak truthfully,
Who hates nought more than clear thinking.   60

SCENE II

MUCH, MOST.

MUCH: Haven't you perchance ever heard
Of the man, being a drunkard,
Whose secret is known to all?
Who goes forever to and fro
Gulping more to drown his sorrow,   65
Forsaking the work he must do?
   'Tis I. But for me no more shame
When I appear and I am seen,
No matter who may moan and groan,
And I fear neither man nor beast.   70
My name is made of endless names;[8]
I soar to be used as shelter,
But my shade is that of the yew;
He who rests beneath in slumber
Will find but grief and misfortune,   75
To suffer endless misery.
I give promises readily,
But he who trusts in my promise
Is deceived: I use treachery,
And my heart is all artifice.   80
   Mine is a most inventive mind,
Whose tireless cogitation
Is aimed at my personal gain.
I answer to admonitions
That it is for the common good,   85
An adequate explanation.
I much revel in my pleasure,
In my wealth and in my glory.
I shall do what no man before
Has done, to live in memory.   90
   Ask each of the simple soldiers
Risking their lives but for silver,
They will tell you who I may be.
Go to the lines of skilled archers,

<pre>
          Where they hoist standards and banners: 95
          Now and then you will find me.
          I shall neither have a master
          Nor serve anyone but myself.
          My right hand is always offered
          To give an oath, and break my word.   100
              I act according to my mood,
          Among the contented and the malcontented,
          With feelings of friendship for none.
          If I hear a contradiction,
          I send my guards and my yeomen   105
          Into battle, mercilessly.
          And to the last, all are punished.
          But should I deal with a grandee,
          Half of my bread will become his;
          Those are the tricks that I can play.   110
MOST: May God keep him for whose glory
          Many a gleaming sword was drawn.
MUCH: May God keep this vision, so fair,
          Whom less I know the more I look.
MOST: Don't you recognize me, my son?   115
          I am Most, your mighty father;
          And you are Much, my creation,
          'Though you preceded me hither.
MUCH: Indeed, I have never seen you:
          I gazed upon your appearance   120
          And expected quite another;
          You have a body, as I do.
MOST: Buried in the depth of your heart
          Lies a pleasure, or a regret,
          About which to all your lips are sealed;   125
          Do reveal to me your secret.
MUCH: I must—it stands to reason—
          Bare my heart to you so fully
          That you may judge if my actions
          Are, in your opinion, worthy.   130
MOST: O such a friend, O such a bond!
          Truly, my son, your heart and mine
          In all ways are one and the same.
</pre>

	It is a wondrous conjunction.	
MUCH:	While I haven't yet seen your own,	135
	I can judge, from its features,	
	That it is similar to mine:	
	This bond surpasses all others.	
MOST:	I love honours, gain and pleasure.	
MUCH:	And I have no other desire.	140
MOST:	I love to be adored on Earth.	
MUCH:	There too I rest my happiness.	
MOST:	I love abundant possessions.	
MUCH:	Those are my very intentions.	
MOST:	I would rather be feared than loved.	145
MUCH:	I, above all, to be esteemed.	
MOST:	No man must feel equal to me.	
MUCH:	It is the sun that I envy.	
MOST:	I want it all while giving nought.	
MUCH:	This is what I always attempt.	150
MOST:	Of wealth I am never sated.	
MUCH:	To have nothing is what I dread.	
MOST:	I like towns, palaces, chateaux.	
MUCH:	Pastimes all, where I long to go.	
MOST:	I like the music cantors sing.	155
MUCH:	There as well I apply my mind.	
MOST:	I love women, good wines, banquets.	
MUCH:	I consider them great assets.	
MOST:	I love to acquire treasures.	
MUCH:	And so do I, or even more.	160
MOST:	I love gems, most rare and precious.	
MUCH:	And I do find them delicious.	
MOST:	I love spun gold, silver, and silk.	
MUCH:	They give my heart a joyful thrill.	
MOST:	I love to build, to have and keep.	165
MUCH:	That is what I most want and seek.	
MOST:	But I love revenge best of all.	
MUCH:	It does much to lighten my heart.	
MOST:	I take great pleasure in treasons.	
MUCH:	So do I, for many reasons.	170
MOST:	I honor a skilled poisoner.	
MUCH:	My possessions are his to share.	

MOST: Astrologers I fully trust.
MUCH: Soothsayers hear all my secrets.[9]
MOST: I fear sadness and malady.   175
MUCH: So does the bold man that I am.
MOST: I fear my being recognized.
MUCH: This fear has never left my side.
MOST: I fear the smallest accidents.
MUCH: Of these fears I have thousands.   180
MOST: I fear the cold, wind, and tempests.
MUCH: I have such a fear in my head.
MOST: All ills and miseries I dread,
          But most of all I do fear Death.
MUCH: My fear of her is horrible,   185
          For above all she's terrible.
MOST: Since we are one like the other,
          Let us now walk together.
MUCH: In your path as well as your way
          I want to stay, so glad am I   190
          To have met a friend such as you.
MOST: But to be approved as is due,
          The truth I must tell in earnest.
MUCH: Do so, for I can hardly wait.
MOST: Lo! What indeed are you wearing?   195
MUCH: Hem! I don't know where that came from.
MOST: Those are ears.
MUCH: No, those are Devils!
MOST: Ears, and they are the most evil
          That any man could ever see.
MUCH: Then I must inform you as well   200
          That quite like mine, so have you.
MOST: What? I have those? Such affliction
          Is quite impossible to bear!
MUCH: We must comfort one another
          And conceal our misfortune.   205
MOST: To have on such a perfect head
          The ears of lowly animals!
MUCH: What shame they will bring upon us
          If people hear about them!
MOST: They must be properly restrained   210

Under a stately cover.
All those bonnets are mine to wear:
Tell me whether those fit me well.
MUCH: Nothing could be better, I feel.
And the same I shall do to mine   215
Under those caps, so we may hide
From others what we are and do.
Do I look right?
MOST: Indeed you do.
MUCH: And so do you. Let us go forth;
And, unsparing of weary feet,   220
We must travel across the land.
MOST: My heart sinks from this too-great pain,
And nothing will lessen my plight.
MUCH: The wealth in which I sought delight
Cannot prevent me from screaming.   225
Should these beastly features be seen,
We shall be mocked by one and all.
MOST: We jointly suffer this evil,
But our power is so great
That if anyone knows of it   230
And whispers but a single word,
We shall see to it that the dolt
Enjoys few chances to chatter.
MUCH: But the truth will be laid bare.
MOST: That it be true doesn't matter.   235
But this truth must remain covered,
And we shall carry it softly.
MUCH: Indeed we suffer grievously
From such an imperfection.
MOST: This is where dissimulation   240
Is for us virtue most sublime.
MUCH: The deed is done, and to kill time,
In the fields let us go walking.
MOST: But who brought here those two, strolling,
Who laugh together constantly?   245
MUCH: Let us listen to what they say.

SCENE III

LITTLE, LESS, MUCH, MOST.

LITTLE: I'm called Little, who always hides;
         I am also, and do not mind,
         Little loved and even less feared.
         I watch over both sheep and cows: 250
         I tie up the swine for slaughter.
         No rest; forever my body
         Is pushed to work. I pay dearly
         For it, for nothing is my own.
         And I have at my side a purse   255
         That's filled with all my possessions.

LESS: Poor Less is the name I'm given,
         The least important of all men;
         Nothing I have, nothing I want.
         From morn to night, with my body,   260
         My feet, my arms, my hands, I work:
         In that I fulfill my wishes.
         No children or nephews to rear,
         No longing to give them riches,
         My fortune is under my hair,   265
         And for my life I have no fear.[10]

LITTLE: Of mine you are.

LESS: Of yours I am.

LITTLE: We are guided all by one thought.

LESS: We walk in complete agreement.

LITTLE: You and I share one sentiment.   270

LESS: The sound of your voice I know well.

LITTLE: And I have long been quite aware
         That such you are and such you were.

LESS: Identical head ornaments
         In similar ways, we carry.   275

LITTLE: We both live in similar hopes,
         Similar aims, similar ends.

LESS: Neither I nor you is clever,
         But the finest we make finer.

LITTLE: And because endlessly we are   280
          Little and Less, so very slight,
          Those with ambitious appetites
          Do not know how to catch us.
LESS: We fear no one coming near us:
          Whenever we walk towards men,   285
          So small are we compared to them
          That they cannot see us at all.
LITTLE: A prudent man must not tempt fate
          If he knows that he might be caught.[11]
LESS: Our garments are so worthless   290
          That if anyone tugs at them
          They most easily turn to shreds,
          And thus we cannot be restrained.
LITTLE: One can't punish the innocent,
          Nor can one touch him who is nought.   295
LESS: But a dead man, whom they reproach
          For all his sins and his misdeeds,
          Will so lightly bear this ordeal
          That he will not deign to reply.
LITTLE: A ewe with no wool can't be shorn;   300
          Own nothing, and nothing you lose.
LESS: Hold nothing, and nothing is seen.
          This will remain a mystery
          To those for whom gain's the query.
LITTLE: They can't find the first end of it,   305
          Yet they think that they have it all.
          But this all that they say is theirs
          Is, in the end, all misfortune.
          Our All is not of that sort.
LESS: Indeed this All must come from nought   310
          In order to be truly loved.
LITTLE: And we find it quite auspicious
          To bear with poverty extreme,
          And to have nought but ourselves.
LESS: But a greater treasure we have   315
          Whose praise we cannot sing higher;
          Our very horns, for their power,
          During all quarrels and disputes

<pre>
             Protect, and surely comfort us.
LITTLE: And they also lavish upon us   320
             The nourishment that we most need.
LESS: We are at last free from blindness
             And the smoky world of darkness.
             In lieu of candles and torches
             We live by the Sun's only light.   325
LITTLE: Verily, the Sun is so bright
             That next to it other fires
             Seem but counterfeit and playthings.
LESS: Thus let us walk in the splendor
             Of our Sun, with much ardor.[12]   330
             Let us be silent, and listen.
LITTLE: Whenever others call us Sheep
             Or the Horned ones, we must be still.
LESS: I learned to play the part quite well.
             But let us walk on, laughing still.   335
             Before we have lived our days,
             He will come, the One who must come.
LITTLE: I cannot control my laughter,
             For my horn promised it to me.
LESS: Horned ones we are, and Friends: 340
             A single heart, a single will.
LITTLE: One Death, and from it but one Health:
             Above all, I long for this Death.
LESS: Alas, I sigh and yearn for it.
MUCH: There, look at him.
MOST: My Faith, that's he.   345
LITTLE: There, look at him.
LESS: He's so wily.
MUCH: I see him.
MOST: And I smell his scent.
MUCH: Yes, more of garlic than incense.
LITTLE: How affable he pretends to be!
LESS: Let us turn there.
LITTLE: No, straight we go.   350
             If he comes to us, let him pass.
MUCH: One must learn to remove the fat
             From waddings of fur and from wool.[13]
</pre>

MOST: I get my furs before winter
          As I do not care to be cold.   355
MUCH: Let us chat with this ragged man:
          He may tell us amusing things.
MOST: Well said!
MUCH: Friend, we would like to learn
          What you do and how you live.
LITTLE: Well, Sir, a simple straw can burn   360
          On its own, without fanning.
LESS: A tall tree is easily felled.
MUCH: Why are you wearing on your heads
          Those horns? They are but for cuckolds.
MOST: Those are to make you more honest;   365
          They also help you hear better.[14]
LESS: Our horns are to defend us,
          And they are neither bone nor flesh.
LITTLE: But of both, do you understand,
          To defend the skin, and the bone.   370
MUCH: They have worn holes into your hats.
LESS: But the hat is thus protected.
MOST: Truly, it is pierced through and through,
          And you are not aware of it.
LITTLE: Its virtue and its great power   375
          Cannot be placed in any ears,
          Even in ears as large as yours
          Might be.
MUCH: And why can't they?
LESS: He is not wise who wants to be.
MOST: Tell us and we shall understand.   380
LITTLE: These horns, and this we shall maintain,
          Deserve to be praised, and more so.
          If a man struck us with a blow
          On the head, he would harm himself,
          And the horn would injure as well   385
          The hand that attempts to hit us.
LESS: It allows us to escape
          Many an evil: between them
          And ourselves it is a wedge.
MUCH: What eggs?

LITTLE: They are large ostrich eggs;   390
          They strike harder than does a log;
          But still the horn shatters them all.
MOST: These are merry fools if their fears
          Are ostrich eggs and those of geese.[15]
MUCH: Why do you show such happiness,   395
          That seems to go on endlessly?
LESS: You could in no way guess of it,
          And as for us, we cannot tell.
MOST: Why?
LITTLE: We would bring you such laughter,
          And would so laugh while we explain,   400
          That no lord, villain, or peasant
          Could ever learn about it.
MUCH: Why?
LESS: We cannot be understood.
          For we laugh so much and so hard,[16]
          That nought but a sound can be heard,   405
          Demonstrating our pleasure.
LITTLE: We lose the strength and the desire
          To speak: befooled by laughter,
          We become unable to speak,
          And can't utter a single word.   410
LESS: Sir, just thinking about it
          Causes me to laugh till I cry.
MOST: You feel neither sorrow nor grief?
LITTLE: We are never displeased or sad.
MUCH: And if you are beaten?
LESS: I laugh,   415
          Because I remember my horn.
LITTLE: Fie upon grief, sad and gloomy!
          Glory be to this little horn.
LESS: Glory to this so charming horn;
          Its story is so full of joy   420
          That it will bring tears of laughter
          To those who attempt to tell it,
          To think of it, or to write it.
          When we presume to say the words,
          We are seized by foolish laughter   425

	That prevents it from being told.	
MOST:	We laugh as well.	
LITTLE:	Yes, with your lips,	

That prevents it from being told.
MOST: We laugh as well.
LITTLE: Yes, with your lips,
But certainly not in your heart.[17]
If you knew, laughter would be yours:
To know it is all that matters.   430
MUCH: Tell us.
LESS: I don't have the power.
MOST: Only a little, to begin.
LITTLE: In the beginning was . . .
I can not go on beyond this.
MUCH: But what is it? Speak, Apostle![18]   435
LESS: Was. . . Ah! I cannot go farther!
MOST: Go ahead: tell us the rest:
Do not make the story so brief.
LITTLE: There was a. . . My faith, I shall burst:
Joy so touches and fills my heart   440
That I am unable to speak.[19]
MUCH: He's laughing so hard that he sweats.
MOST: He should hold a jester's bauble,
For more of a fool there is none.
MUCH: Come here. What is your opinion   445
Of us? Look at our faces.
LESS: You are persons of importance,
So high that I dare not approach
And come near you, or even touch
Your robes that are too precious.   450
LITTLE: Yes indeed, the work is gorgeous;
See the elegant needlework.
MOST: He calls work this unusual craft:
It is pursing, edging, trimming,
And embroidery, with ruffling—   455
All done in gold, silver and silk.
MUCH: Are you scoffing?[20]
LESS: I laugh for joy.
MOST: To have seen such costly garments?
LITTLE: No, for what is missing from them.
MUCH: Our robes are perfect, truly.   460
LESS: A single horn, very simply,

<pre>
                Is needed to make them perfect.
MOST: Let us make him happy. In fact,
                You see, we do carry a horn.
                This one is from the unicorn,   465
                Against all poisons and the plague.
MUCH: And here is some of what is left
                From the antlers of a great beast,
                The stag, that wherever it is,
                Protects from thunder and lightning.[21]   470
                Are you laughing?
LESS: Laughing to tears.
                My God! Do you feel no shame
                To so ignore the great story
                That, as we do, would make you laugh?
MOST: Horns we do have (can't you see?)   475
                That are beautiful and worthy.
LESS: They will have to carry tapers,
                Since they can protect from evil.[22]
LITTLE: Do they protect you from dying?
MUCH: Nay.
LESS: But ours do so indeed,   480
                For they are more worthy than yours.
                Whenever Death approaches us,
                She is so afraid to get caught
                Upon our horns, that she flees!
                She dreads them, and thus it follows   485
                That free from her power, we live.
MOST: We find your horns unattractive.
                They also seem too cumbersome.
LITTLE: But to us they are so winsome
                That we don't value yours at all.   490
MUCH: We set ours in precious gems
                With gold and silver, and we drink
                The water in which we place them
                To cure all our illnesses.[23]
MOST: Those are the old horns of a sheep.   495
                They are worthless—nothing but filth.
LESS: If I had told you the story
                Of my horn and its history,
</pre>

Never again could you believe
That any other is worthy. 500
And when I think of it again,
My unceasing laughter returns.
MUCH: What reason?
LITTLE: The story is
So pleasing, so delectable,
That even Acteon's fable 505
Of antlers, on which you tarry,
Is nothing compared to ours.[24]
And the story told by Pliny
Of the fair unicorn so rare
That must be caught by a maiden 510
Is far from equalling ours.[25]
LESS: These stories may be told in words
But they cannot rival ours,
Of which no one dares to speak.
MOST: We know nothing of it.
LITTLE: We regret 515
To keep it secret, both for us
And for you as well.
MUCH: What is this?
First, you make us long to hear it,
Then speak not a word.
LESS: Telling it
Would greatly lessen our lives. 520
MOST: Does this story make you happy?
LITTLE: Happy? Sated with happiness.
MUCH: Such laughter I have never seen.
For laughter they should win the prize.
MOST: So different are we, alas, 525
From their manners and from their means!
LESS: I am so very drunk with bliss,
That laughing is all I can do.
MUCH: We have far better things to do:
We have responsibilities.[26] 530
LITTLE: Yes, by the Grace of God, I see,
You are blessed with honors and wealth;
And you seem endowed with good health,

	Seeing your rosy complexion.	
MOST:	(*Aside*.) He can't see our affliction,	535
	Or where the shoe pinches now.	
LESS:	The calf that is inside a cow	
	Can't be seen until it comes forth.	
MUCH:	None of our constant efforts	
	Can hide these endless ears of ours.	540
LITTLE:	This should not displease you at all:	
	For if they are truly bigger,	
	You must hear better and know more	
	Than perhaps could anyone else?	
MOST:	Midas, Midas, Midas, Midas![27]	545
	All your sorrows are beyond peer.	
LESS:	Do they give you much pain, those ears,	
	That cause you to cry and lament?	
MUCH:	None but their stubborn reluctance	
	To remain under my bonnet.	550
LITTLE:	But it is not wise, I suggest,	
	To conceal what should be revealed.	
MOST:	I can bear the constant ordeal	
	Of wearing hats, nightcaps, and hoods.	
	But with ears of such magnitude	555
	I have no choice but to wear them.	
LESS:	Have you no control over them?	
MOST:	Far less than would a servitor.	
	I am the unwilling bearer,	
	And my ears are lord and master.	560
MUCH:	Alas, how much displeasure	
	Born from them is relentlessly	
	Imposed upon us more each day!	
	It is a too-uncertain pain.	
LITTLE:	If he felt neither love nor hate	565
	For all things but horns, as we do,	
	He would not feel such great sorrow.	
MOST:	Alas, Alas, Alas, Alas!	
MUCH:	Midas, Midas, Midas, Midas,	
	In your name we endure such pain!	570
MOST:	And our pain is much in vain	
	For we cannot truly devise	

          The way to fashion a disguise,
          To protect those ears from all eyes.
MUCH: In our hearts there is no joy,   575
          No matter how we may appear;
          Our hearts are consumed with fear:
          Our lives are most unhappy.
LESS: But filled with triumph and glory,
          Seeing your garments and your pomp.   580
LITTLE: Don't you ever play at spinning tops,[28]
          And hitting them hard with a whip?
          It would be much comfort for you
          For want of better exercise.
LESS: It seems to me at first sight that   585
          There is nothing wrong with your ears.
          They are, one against the other,
          Both healthy and clean.
MUCH: Yes indeed:
          But won't you at least concede
          How big they are?
LITTLE: Be patient!   590
          Must you for so little lament,
          Since you have all that you may need?
MOST: Alas, riches are worth nothing,
          As they disturb and cause us harm;
          For under this cap, day or night,   595
          I cannot tuck them both away.
MUCH: When I think of their ugliness
          Nowhere can I find contentment.
LESS: And in your beautiful garment
          Don't you find pleasure or glory?   600
MOST: No, for of my ears the memory
          Brings me vexation and sorrow;
          It is a hard pill to swallow.
MUCH: 'Tis for us a cruel repast.
MOST: Midas, Midas, Midas, Midas,   605
          You were born to mortify us.
LITTLE: If it pleases you, your Highness
          (I do not know what to call you),
          Would it perhaps satisfy you

<pre>
          To speak to us, in part at least,   610
          Of your troubles?
LESS: We may assist,
          If we can find a remedy.
MUCH: To speak of them is agony!
          That story is so pitiful,
          Its memory is so awful,   615
          That to tell it we have no terms.
MOST: One can only write it with tears;
          One can only tell it with shouts.
MUCH: So pathetic are their accounts
          That they cannot be recited.   620
MOST: I am by them more incited
          To weep out of compassion
          Than I would by the passion
          Of Jesus or that of his Saints.
LITTLE: (Aside.) Something is amiss in their brains,   625
          And their minds wander far too much.
LESS: Won't you at least share it with us,
          To cheer you and lessen your pain?
MUCH: No, for we have to suffer them,
          But were it not that to hide them   630
          Is far beyond our power,
          We would not mention them.
LITTLE: Your cap
          Should cover them.
MOST: When one slips back,
          The other refuses to stay.
MUCH: On account of them, my bonnets   635
          Will not stay upon my head.
LESS: As for me, I find them most fair;
          If only what they are lacking
          Were there as well.
MOST: What?
LESS: What they need
          Is horns, as graceful ornaments.   640
LITTLE: The horn by its simple presence
          Would upon your ears bring honor.
MUCH: It would attract the eye further
</pre>

	To what we want to keep secret.	
LESS:	But if the horn is bound to it,	645
	You will be spared from all who mock.	
LITTLE:	You will suddenly see it shock	
	Those who, by mocking, are shockers.	
MOST:	I have no fear but of mockers,	
	For I only prize my honor.	650
LESS:	And the rejoicing in one's heart,	
	Have you no regard for it, Sir?	
MUCH:	I am so far from it: I sigh,	
	Alas, for it cannot be mine.	
LITTLE:	Why?	
MUCH:	For this dilemma of mine	655
	To hide these burdensome ears.	
LESS:	They may possibly be so dense[29]	
	That through them you cannot hear well.	
MOST:	What I hear from them brings no joy	
	And no pleasure: to the center	660
	Of my heart the pain enters,	
	And it comes from these too-large ears.	
LITTLE:	Have you nothing to dry those tears?	
	Gather round some story-tellers.	
MUCH:	We do have numerous jesters,	665
	Whose sayings are admirable!	
LESS:	Don't you find them agreeable?	
MOST:	Yes, pleasing to the ears, somewhat,	
	But they fan in a burning heart	
	The sorrow born of their sayings:	670
	For not all is to its liking,	
	And in this we can't find pleasure.	
MUCH:	The more we try to pull them off,	
	The more diligent our efforts,	
	The more increases our pain,	675
	And thus all efforts are in vain.	
LITTLE:	What if you were to cut them off?	
MOST:	We were quite eager to do so:	
	But they are one with our lives,	
	That we would lose by losing them.	680
LESS:	You say your lives depend on them?	

In earnest, you are mistaken:
'Tis your death that they will hasten,
Since they make you cry night and day.
MUCH: It was of no purpose to pray   685
To doctors, both living and dead,
Taking potions so highly praised,
And all cures imaginable,
Just to make them invisible;
None of this provided a cure.   690
MOST: These people, so needy and poor,
Are far more content than we are.
LITTLE: Devils or men we do not fear
Nor do we an inconstant Fate.
LESS: She does not affect our health.   695
Be it hot or cold, we are hale.
MUCH: But must you not work with your hands?
LITTLE: Yes, but our minds are at ease,
And in all things they find delight,
For the horn pierces through their hearts.   700
MOST: Truly you are but a liar,
For upon your head I see it.
LITTLE: But in my heart I do feel it:
I myself feel it in my heart.
MORE: If ever there were Innocents,   705
Those two are: I grant them the name.[30]
MOST: But as simple fools I rank them
Among the nicest I have ever seen.
LESS: And you remain wise at all times?
MUCH: And you will be fools and lowly.   710
LITTLE: Yes, we shall live as we fancy;
You will be wise and glorious:
But your hearts would be joyous
If you felt, as we do, pleasure.
LESS: For all, there is only one Sun: 715
One is black, and the other white.[31]
MOST: Ah, let us proceed in order.
Would you toss all things together?
LITTLE: I laugh so, that I can't answer,
Because my horn fears no ill wind.   720

MUCH: But why such laughter?
MOST: Do go on!
          You do too well as what you are![32]
          But like full holy-water fonts
          Our hearts weep with bitter tears.
LITTLE: Haven't you asked the she-gossips,[33]   725
          Who know so many good sayings?
MUCH: But you are such fools, I think,
          That you would not dare speak to them.
LESS: We do, and hide nothing from them:
          But when we speak we always laugh.   730
MUCH: And we cry when we implore them,
          For we are too often denied.
LITTLE: Thus you deceive and use women,
          Adoring them as images.
MOST: The more paint is on their faces,   735
          The more our hearts are smitten
          By their so fair complexion.
MUCH: The words from their vermilion lips
          Oftentimes flow in our ears
          Until they are thoroughly filled.[34]   740
LESS: Your rejoicing is thus fulfilled
          When you hear words soft as spun-silk;
          Seeing beauty at its highest,
          You should know pleasure as we do.
MOST: All this turns to pain and sorrow   745
          And fills one's heart with much torment.
LITTLE: Have you no source of merriment?
          Do you not hunt, and go hawking,
          Jousting, singing, hopping, dancing,
          Or other pastimes, all pleasant?   750
MUCH: That makes us far more discontented,
          For all too soon all turns to grief;
          And our pleasure is so brief
          That we question its existence.
LESS: Alleluya, Alleluya,   755
          In pleasure you find misery?
MOST: And you?
LITTLE: In every torment, glee:

Our horns give solace and peace.
MUCH: Ah, for every joy our ears
        Bring us a myriad of sorrows.   760
LESS: In multi-hued fields and meadows,
        In rivers, in forests, in streams,
        In commons, in parks, in gardens,
        In your castles and your mansions,
        In glorious ornamentation,   765
        Do you find no consolation?
MUCH: Midas, Midas, Midas, Midas
        Has robbed us of all contentment.
MOST: And the cost is exorbitant:
        He turns our wealth into woes.   770
LITTLE: And all our travails and cares
        Our horn turns into blessings.
MUCH: They seem happier with nothing
        Than we are from having all things.
LESS: Could you not find the very root   775
        Of your plight, to pull it out?
MOST: Alas, we pay dearly the costs
        For each day of peace and repose!
LITTLE: Take pleasure in our discourse
        And laugh!
MOST: Alas, laugh I will not;   780
        As to be merry, I cannot,
        No matter what may come to pass.
LESS: If you would ever so briefly
        Allow my horns inside your ears,
        You would at last find blissful cheer.   785
        Can you bear it for a moment?
MOST: Yes. . . Alas I cannot go on;
        The pain it causes is extreme!
LITTLE: You would know happiness supreme
        If you showed a little patience.   790
MUCH: I must indeed try this science:
        Insert this horn of yours right here.
LITTLE: This I can do.
MUCH: Mercy, Mercy!
        Such torment I cannot endure.

LESS: This pain may be your only cure,   795
           And you demur and refuse it?
MOST: One cannot possibly use it:
           We do not have such puissance.
LITTLE: You would gain from it the knowledge
           Of the great story and its glee.   800
MUCH: It would be a great mockery
           To pay attention to these fools.
MOST: Tired we are, and not grateful.
           Of horns we want to hear no more.
           And ears, from which we much suffer,   805
           Are far from so sharply pointed.
LESS: They are suitable and needed;
           Without them your life is filled
           With misery; and die you will
           Sadly, your eyes brimming with tears.   810
MUCH: Our sorrow will be concealed
           Amidst pastimes and distractions.
MOST: And the source of my affliction,
           These very ears, I shall cover
           With the jewels from my treasure   815
           To conceal them.
MUCH: I, with bonnets,
           With caps, with masks, and with collars,
           With hoods, with kerchiefs and mufflers.
LITTLE: We need not cover our horns:
           To show them is our desire.   820
MUCH: Velvet in such amounts we tear,
           So much brocade and cloth of gold,
           That their openings will be closed;
           Indeed too wide and large they gape.
MOST: And to better conceal their shape,   825
           We spare neither cloth nor spun gold,
           Neither veils, hats, nightcaps or hoods,
           Nor small bonnets, handsome and new,
           Not just one, two, or a dozen:
           Hundreds, to better subdue them.   830
MUCH: And of bonnets, these four, I hope,
           Are enough to make them a cope.

MOST: By my word, it is all in vain.
           What a pity!
MUCH: And a great shame!
MOST: It is a bitter experience.   835
           What should we do, you happy men?
LESS: Nought, but for a moment to suffer
           Of our horn the great power.
MUCH: 'Tis impossible. Have you not
           A more feasible remedy?   840
LITTLE: To the impossible, they say,
           All remedies are found wanting.
           Roland we are not, or daring.
           Of things new we are not aware.
LESS: To us, all things are good and fair.   845
MOST: To us, evil, ugly, and foul;
           And as a cure all charms and spells
           Have been so far to no avail.
LITTLE: But should you agree to submit
           (If only for a few minutes)   850
           To keeping the horn in your ear,
           We are certain, and it is clear,
           That you would at last find and own
           The happiness that we have found.
MUCH: But we cannot endure its pain,   855
           And we prefer the pain we bear
           Rather than submit our heads
           To foolish horns, for such torment.
LESS: But you cannot without them
           Be happy.
MOST: Thus we shall remain   860
           Forever sad, and die we shall
           Of grief, rather than to endure,
           Because of the horns, such torture
           As we were beginning to feel.
MUCH: It is to liberate the Soul   865
           From the body.
LITTLE: I must confess
           That they cause torment and distress
           Almost beyond man's endurance.

	But their torment is within bounds,	
	And it never leads to despair.	870
MOST:	Such pain we simply cannot bear.	
LESS:	If in its joy you could believe,	
	This pain you would gently receive,	
	And accept it with gratitude.	
MUCH:	We can't understand a pleasure	875
	That begins with such suffering.	
LITTLE:	Of a simple creature the ears	
	Cannot perceive or comprehend	
	The great pleasure that is given	
	By the horns that we hold so dear.	880
LESS:	Let us leave, lest we disquiet	
	These men, others, or ourselves.	
MOST:	Here we remain, sad and ashen,	
	Lamenting, weeping and crying.	
LITTLE:	And we wend our way, laughing,	885
	As we know that so swiftly ends	
	The journey from morning to night,	
	And that very soon we shall rest.	
LESS:	In his repose finds much delight	
	He who has labored well and long.	890
MUCH:	And he who is inside a tomb,	
	Is he, do tell, much gratified?	
LITTLE:	I fear neither ice nor fire,	
	I fear neither death nor disease.	
MOST:	And yet (no matter what one says)	895
	Being is what matters.	
LESS:	Well said.	
MUCH:	I mean: being happy and rich,	
	With all of one's wishes fulfilled.	
LITTLE:	But we have all pleasures and say	
	That there is nothing but being.	900
MOST:	Being what?	
LESS:	At any window,	
	Watching the fine season draw near,	
	Living from the joyful memory	
	Of our horns so filled with love.	
MUCH:	These wearisome ears of ours	905

Cause us to be filled with languor,
And we feel the constant sorrow
To see of those ears the shadow.
MOST: Our ills are in such number
 That they can be called endless, 910
 And I dread the sight of Devils,
 For all the joys of Paradise
 Cannot prevent these cursed woes.
MUCH: Great fear assails us from all sides,
 But most within us, doubt it not, 915
 For the deluge is in our hearts.
 Lest others pass judgement on us,
 Let us leave, for that is enough.
LESS: Pray God for all the departed,
 Whose return is not to be known. 920
LITTLE: Some did return, it is written,
 But very few: the road is long.[35]
LESS: Gentle horns on our forehead,
 Let us go and rest together.
LITTLE: Let us, that our time be not wasted. 925

NOTES TO *MOST, MUCH, LITTLE, LESS*

1. John, XXII:46.

2. 2nd Book of Samuel, XXII:3.

3. Enigmas were a popular form of entertainment, and numerous authors included in their works poems in the form of an enigma. A few are simple, but others defy the most arduous efforts to decipher their obscure clues (e.g., among Marguerite's, *Enigme*, p. 282, *Les Marguerites de la Marguerite des Princesses*, Carnet du Bibliophile, Tome IV, 1873).

4. Quoting Montaiglon, Saulnier explains that shady characters would shoot unsuspecting passers-by or selected victims through holes in walls behind which they remained hidden. In other words, those who, being

his people or working for him, know Most's identity, are spies, hypocrites, and cowards. A sarbacane is a blow-tube or pipe for shooting with.

5.   A clear allusion to torture and death at the stake. One hears in this passage an echo of *The Inquisitor*.

6.   Perhaps symbolic of the Faculty of Theology of the University of Paris and of the Parlement.

7.   Gloves, hats, capes and elegant clothes are symbols of power and of the luxury of the high clergy: again, an echo of *The Inquisitor*.

8.   This alliteration on the word "nom, noms, sans nombre" in French suggests that we are not dealing with one individual but with a large number of persons with similar philosophies and enjoying the same protection of anonymity.

9.   Saulnier duly noted Marguerite's criticism of soothsaying and astrology, and also condemned in the *Comedy for Four Women*. We must add that Louise of Savoy, the author's mother, had a physician-astrologer in residence. Marguerite did not.

10.   His fortune "under his hair" is the horns that have not yet been mentioned.

11.   Little, more cautious than Less, wants to stay out of harm's way by avoiding the powerful Most and Much.

12.   Lines 325, 326, 330: As Saulnier points out, these are direct allusions to the Gospel. The Sun is emblematic of the law of God (Psalm XIX), the presence of God (Psalm LXXXIV), the person of the Savior (John I:9 and Malachi IV:2), the purity of heavenly beings (Revelations).

13.   Much and Most pretend to chat idly, but Much reveals their desire to gain from every possible source of profit, even the poorest, such as extracting fat from the fur of short-haired animals before tanning the skin for leather.

14.   Most assumes that their horns are a form of punishment, of humiliation. His second thought is, of course, that they are used for spying. There may be a reference to the use of horns as ear-trumpets, but it is not clear when this practice began.

15.   Lines 389-90 contain an untranslatable pun: "eux" (them) and "oeufs" (eggs), leading to "autruche" (ostrich) and Autriche (Austria), Rome's ally. In Most's reply, the ostrich, now associated with Austria, is placed side by side with the goose, a well-known symbol of stupidity.

16.   In the French the four syllables "tant, tant et tant" are linked into one continuous sound evoking endless laughter. This is the rapture experienced by the Shepherdess (*Comedy of Mont de Marsan*), Amarissima (*Comedy on the Passing of the King*), and various others in Marguerite's plays.

17.   The French "rire des dents" used here means a forced laugh, or polite laughter hiding one's true feelings.

18.   As Saulnier pointed out, line 433 is the beginning of the Gospel according to St. John. Consequently, Much (who knows the Scriptures) will ironically urge: "Parlez, Apostre!" (Go on, Apostle!) when Little stops speaking.

19.   Again, they are too enraptured to speak further. By the same token, one may not, but Marguerite may be suggesting that they do not dare to quote the Scriptures in French, since translating them from Latin was forbidden by law.

20.   It is known that Marguerite frowned on excess: she usually wore a black velvet garment with simple fur lining, which, in *La Coche*, she gleefully but wickedly contrasts with the sartorial extravagance of her brother's mistress.

21.   What Most and Much carry is *ground* horn, then considered a great antidote for all known diseases. This causes Little and Less to laugh even harder.

22.   A clear satire on the tapers that are placed before the images of saints in churches for forgiveness or to enhance a prayer.

23.   Marguerite is probably alluding to the elaborate decorations of statues and reliquaries in Roman churches.

24.   Saulnier refers to Ovid's *Metamorphoses*, I, 3. Acteon the hunter was transformed into a stag and devoured by his dogs after seeing Diana bathing. Clearly, this tale is a poor example as to the value of horns for protection!

25.   The unicorn, whose legend was known since antiquity, was a popular subject for tapestries and paintings. In medieval France the ground horn of the unicorn was considered a much-valued (and costly) antidote for poison. It had lost some of its popularity by the end of the sixteenth century.

26.   This remark recalls Calvin's criticism of Marguerite's entourage. Saulnier suggests that Dolet's famous "Vivent les enfants sans souci!" is the key to much of this play; hence Much's pompous and

self-important "Nous ne sommes pas sans souci" (We are not without cares, we have responsibilities).

27.   Lines 545, 568, 569, 605: Following the comical lamentations (Midas, Midas) and (Alas, Alas) the roles are temporarily suspended: Most and Much, no longer condescending, speak openly of their troublesome ears, whose virtues Little and Less, no longer fearful, calmly discuss.

28.   "Jouer aux trompes" was a game in which players whipped a small wooden top to make it spin and keep it spinning; hence the proverb "il n'a pas le fouet pour mener cette trompe" (he is not equipped for such a project) (used in a sexual context in the XVIth century). The game was later called "jouer au sabot"; it was not a competetive game. On the other hand, "jouer aux toupies," also translated as the game of tops, was a totally different game: each player had a top that he threw (already spinning) to knock those of others out of the game. The last spinning top won the game.

29.   This is a play on the words "lourdes," and "sourdes," which can mean "heavy, dense" as well as "deaf."

30.   "Innocent" has several meanings in French: (1) free from guilt ("Les Saints-Innocents" were the children slain upon King Herod's order); (2) simple-minded, childlike; (3) mentally retarded (the "village idiot" has always been called "l'innocent du village").

31.   Saulnier interprets this cryptic metaphor thus: all four men have the same God; for two, it is the God of the Sorbonne (black); for the others, it is the God of Meaux (white). I think that Less refers to death, which is for him the way to eternal life and the already mentioned pure light, while it is terrifying darkness for Most and Much.

32.   As fools, who laugh mindlessly.

33.   Commères: women who gossip and dispense advice as well as folk remedies. While Saulnier's note suggests that Little praises their wisdom, I read Little's remark as ironic. He and Less speak to the women, but do not take their advice and would have no use for their remedies.

34.   The image of "painted women" suggests the lavish decor of the Catholic Church, which hides the natural simplicity of its edifice, and to the lengthy sermons in which the Scriptures cannot be found.

35.   This is a direct allusion to the Resurrection of Christ and of a few others, such as Lazarus. Saulnier also reports the following words spoken by Marguerite to those who spoke to her of eternal life as she lay dying: "Yes, that is true, but we spend a long time dead and in the ground before it happens", which echoes line 922.

COMEDY ON
THE PASSING OF THE KING

(Comédie sur le trespas du Roy)

INTRODUCTION

Synopsis

Amarissima, alone, weeps at the news of Pan's death. She is joined by her grieving husband Securus, a shepherd, who attempts to end the flow of her tears. A second shepherd, Agape, who had been with Pan at the time of his death, laments his loss. They hear each other's song of sorrow and thus Agape joins Amarissima and Securus. Paraclesis, sent by Pan, brings to them the message of consolation that they need to hear, and they offer a grateful paean to Pan's eternal life.

History and Comments

As its title indicates, this play was written in 1547, after the death of the king of France. As she had done after the death of her niece Charlotte and that of her infant son, Marguerite again turned to poetry and wrote a religious meditation on death and redemption. However, the loss of her beloved brother was far more devastating than any of those she had suffered before. The most cherished (and no doubt most demanding) person in her life, the one whose approval and support she most needed, the one whose love for her she never doubted—the lusty image of strength and of life which towered over her was gone.

In December 1546, François had requested her presence at court, but he was still thought to be in good health and, anxious as she may have been to see him, she had postponed her departure: that winter was unusually harsh, the journey would have been long and taxing, and she was tired. Ailing, saddened by emotional disappointments and financial difficulties, it is only in March that she left to join him, but at the monastery of Tusson, where she stopped to rest, she learned that "the king had died between the hours of one and two in the afternoon, on Thursday, the 31st of March" in Rambouillet. Grief and an intense feeling of guilt must have overwhelmed Marguerite: her brother was dead, and she had not been by his side during his last moments. Neither did she attend the traditional funeral service at Notre-Dame de Paris on May 23rd,[1] remaining in semi-seclusion in Tusson until late July. Those few months can be counted among the most prolific of her literary career, but one must agree with V.L. Saulnier and others that the *Comedy on the Passing of the King* was probably written (or at least completed) after her departure from Tusson.

This is one of those rare instances in which one may be certain that a work is autobiographical. The great Pan, needless to say, is the late king of France, ruler and shepherd to his flock. Amarissima is the expression of Marguerite's suffering and of her despair. Securus, her husband, also quite distressed by Pan's death, and most concerned about Amarissima's desire to mourn him in seclusion, is clearly Henri de Navarre trying to coax her into returning home—a greater effort than she could manage at this point. Agape, according to Saulnier, is Marguerite's nephew Henri, the new ruler of France.

There is documented evidence that François spoke at length to his only surviving son a few hours before his death, but Henri was far from being his favorite offspring and does not appear to have been particularly worthy of the name "beloved." Furthermore, one may wonder whether Henri II, who showed little warmth toward his aunt and even mocked her at court on at least one occasion, shed many a tear upon his father's demise: he never truly forgave those responsible for the four unhappy years that, as a child, he spent in Spain as hostage to secure his father's release and to guarantee that the terms of the treaty with the Emperor would be followed. Although one may wish that Agape had been a beloved member of Marguerite's entourage who happened to be at Court when her brother died, the text leaves no room for doubt: she alludes, perhaps charitably but also coyly (since she and Henri de Navarre desperately needed the funds allocated to her by the French Crown), to the new ruler, her nephew. This diplomatic detail in itself confirms that the play can only have been completed and polished after she had returned to Navarre, that is to say when, time passing, her deep Evangelical beliefs made it possible for her to accept her brother's death, thus to surmount her grief, and to contemplate her now uncertain future.

We may wonder if a new feeling of vulnerability prompted her to offer in Latin her only quotation from the Scriptures. Although quoting the Scriptures in French was strictly forbidden by law, she had done so often and with obvious impunity in the past.

Moreover, it may not be altogether coincidental that in this case she chose an excerpt from the Book of Job.

Evangelism had been both the bane and the source of strength of her life. Many of those who shared her beliefs and whom she attempted to protect suffered emprisonment, torture, or death by burning. Their legacy was the conviction that the death of the body is not to be mourned because it leads to true life if one is worthy of redemption. V.L. Saulnier stresses that Marguerite's first great spiritual leader, the Bishop of Meaux and leader of its Cénacle, insisted on the image of God as the Good Shepherd and that of the faithful as his flock, his sheep. Marguerite wrote of herself as the "lost or wandering ewe" seeking her way to Him. Not only was Pan—the name she gives her brother in this play, and a name given to him in his lifetime on numerous occasions[2]—the great shepherd, the music-loving god symbolizing every element of pastoral life, but he was also the god of the shepherds of Arcadia. According to Plutarch, the news of his death was mysteriously heard all over the land, and instantly followed by a chorus of lamentations. In the opening lines of this play, Amarissima (as had Marguerite herself, unable at first to accept a death that she had dreaded but that she had not seen with her own eyes) challenges the veracity of what she has heard, hoping that it is not so.

In spite of its title and its pastoral setting, and in view of the fact that songs of varying meter are interpolated into the entirely decasyllabic dialogue, this *comédie* is certainly neither an eclogue nor a true comedy. It is more of a lyrical lamentation on death and a prayer for redemption, in which the religious songs, some sung as solos, others as duets or trios, reinforce the recitative. Among the songs that all four characters sing we find several of the *Chansons Spirituelles* written by Marguerite on secular melodies, before and after her brother's death. Keeping in mind that the author has very daringly made of the paraclete (Parakletos, the strengthener, comforter, intercessor, a uniquely masculine symbol) a female role, we hear a quartet with two male and two female voices.[3] We have already noted that this remarkable and noble work is neither a comedy nor an eclogue. Indeed, it is not a dirge nor a lamentation. For want of a more suitable name, one may call it a "favola pastorale," since it involves a dramatic plot as well as a pastoral theme. At the risk of offending experts in music, I suggest that, no matter what Marguerite's intentions were, her play is a precursor of the oratorio, and that, had it been written fifty years later, this is perhaps what it would have been called.[4]

Marguerite has been accused of writing too fast, and indeed as far as "pièces de circonstance" are concerned, it appears that a few of her plays were hurriedly put together. This is far from the case for this work. She clearly intended it to be a fitting tribute to her brother's memory and all indications are that she gave much thought to minute details, such as the building of a two-level stage with, most likely, a backdrop or painted cloth showing, at the top, the house of Securus and Amarissima, and below, a steep downward path with a crossroad at which stood a large cross. Agape's remark reveals that Securus is on a higher plane than he is, and asks for guidance on how to reach him. For the sake of realism, we must assume that the road was simply painted on the backdrop and that the character of Agape, at ground level, walked to the edge of the stage, climbed behind the scenery and reappeared at the upper level, where the characters of Amarissima and Securus stood all along. However, when Securus advises him that to join them he must follow the difficult way of the cross, Agape vouches that he has never taken his eyes from it, and adds that its symbol in his heart gives him strength. Marguerite may be subtly hinting to the new king that ruling is an arduous and demanding task for which he needs divine guidance and a demonstration of true Christian spirit, but one should certainly not read into this admonition a breach of protocol on her part: antagonizing her vindictive nephew would have been most unwise.

Whether this play was performed or not, it appears that this is the unique example of a somewhat elaborate stage set to be found among her seven plays. She also selected with utmost care the names given to her characters. From Pan to Paraclesis and from Amarissima to Agape, these names are either linked to antiquity or to the Scriptures, or they are agnomens, thus all are timeless. Moreover, a simple pastoral setting and traditional shepherds' clothes preclude any suggestion of time or of place. Why such attention to details? Marguerite clearly wanted to sing her brother's fame for posterity at the same time as she lamented and yet celebrated his death. Saulnier names a few of those eloquent masters of rhetoric[5] in whose works (complaints, lamentations, deplorations) she found models that she could follow and imitate. She may have learned from their skill, their technique, their eloquence, their familiarity with the classics. What is striking, and uniquely hers, is the unmistakable authenticity of her feelings and of her emotions. Her original reaction of anger toward fate, her resentment when others try to stop her tears and to pull her from her self-imposed solitude are very real and, being universally experienced, thus understood and shared, they are infinitely touching.

The *Comedy on the Passing of the King* reflects the healing process of catharsis for its author, but here Marguerite has accomplished far more than taming and accepting her grief: she has transformed her sorrow and consolation into a universal statement that transcends personal pathos.

COMEDY ON THE PASSING OF THE KING

(Comédie sur le trespas du Roy)

Amarissima   Securus
Agape, shepherd   Paraclesis

SCENE I

AMARISSIMA.

AMARISSIMA: But is it true, can we know for certain
     That from us on this earth, Pan was taken?
     Alas, truly unfathomable pain!
     But is it true he was torn from us to Heaven?
     'Tis true. Oh, eyes of mine, wilfully blind,   5
     That want to see this mundane world no more,
     Accept, betrayed, the denied torment,
     Do as you must and cry a flood of tears.
     Now from us all, his loving shepherds,
     Has been taken all good and all pleasure,   10
     The protection from evil and dangers.
     From the wolf who could never capture
     A single lamb, for Pan liked nought better
     Than to keep watch on his flock and his land,
     For when he resorted to harsh measures[6]   15
     'Twas to save them from war, secure and sound.
     Because I'll see this gracious god no more,
     To plunge to the depth of my agony,
     I have chosen a secluded abode
     In which this grief of mine I shall sing   20
     In free and total isolation,
     Released from all pleasures and all cares,
     For, losing all, I have no volition,
     And my grief has no need but for tears.

This forsaken site I have chosen for my cries,   25
Abandoning shepherds in their meadows.
I hate the woods, greenery and flowers,
Meads and brooks, castles, cities and towers.
But since death can play such heartless deceits
And spares not the leader of all shepherds,   30
I shall wear black instead of finery—
Yet not so black as is my misery.
Abandon all hopes of consoling me;
Without you, nightingale, linnet or lark,
I want to bear my grief with no reprieve,   35
Until my body is reduced to dust.
I ask of you, oh limpid brooks, to still
The gentle sound that lulled me to sleep,
For ev'ry time I close my weary eyes
I think of my misfortune and I weep.   40
Oh feeble voice, forsaking all music,
Be loud and cry my suffering, alone,
Let sorrow and love be your rhetoric.
Sing verses of pain and desolation,
Words assembled in absence of reason   45
By a mind eternally mortified.
Bring to the firmament the awareness
That he and you were greatly wronged by death.[7]

(*She sings.*)

Alas, I am so unhappy[8]
That I can't tell my misery   50
Indeed I am without hope:
Despair is knocking at my door
And will push me into the depth
From which one can never escape.

SCENE II

SECURUS, AMARISSIMA.

SECURUS: Oh Pan, oh Pan, my master and my friend,   55
          You have been wrenched from our loving sight,
          And in the earth your body is asleep.
          All that is good has with you disappeared.
          What is my sad and grieving heart to do
          But weep, all earthly pleasures forsaken?   60
          I have fastened my lute to the willow,
          Never to hear its melody again.
AMARISSIMA: (*She sings.*) My eyes have shed so many tears,
          No earth nor heaven can they see,
          For they weep in such abundance.   65
          My lips lament eternally,
          And my heart is filled aplenty
          With sighs, without deliverance.
SECURUS: Could it be that I heard the voice so faint
          Of the sorrowful Amarissima,   70
          To whom my hurried steps were leading me?
          Hearing it, I fear that she is near death,
          From head to toe, overwrought with sadness.
          I have heard the song of her great despair;
          In rhyme or in prose, to cry her distress   75
          Is her rightful claim: all is lost for her.
AMARISSIMA: (*She sings.*) Sadness, this insidious power,
          Has made my body grow so weak
          That it has no strength or vigor.
          It might as well be with the dead   80
          Inasmuch as from its appearance
          Many fail to recognize it.
SECURUS: Forsake the song and the tearful sorrow
          That are poison to all bodies and souls,
          My most excellent friend, so dear to me.   85
AMARISSIMA: Oh Securus, true and charitable,
          So deep is my grief, and unbearable,
          That no words will ever console me.

SECURUS: Alas! I know that this is all too true.
    Indeed, wherever I am, I shall rue   90
    Forever this irreplaceable loss.
    You and I have drunk this too-bitter draught:
    Thus, join me in my desolate abode,
    And we'll offer our laments to the gods.
AMARISSIMA: Gentle friend, forsake the forsaken one,   95
    Whom Death has nearly drawn to herself
    When from me she took Pan, my only good.
    I am too overwhelmed with suffering:
    Your house would be ill-suited to my mood,
    Because for me life has lost all meaning.   100
SECURUS: Could you, my dear companion, abandon
    Our flock, to wander in the mountains
    In great danger of the wolf and the bear?
AMARISSIMA: That my face may be ever bathed with tears,
    I claim as my due, my privilege,   105
    For death has preyed upon me too harshly.
SECURUS: I do so not to end your tears,
    Because I too bear a grief most sincere:
    This being so, we may weep together.
AMARISSIMA: Dear one, my love for you is deep and true.   110
    From this retreat I shall depart, and vow
    That death alone can sever my heart from yours.
SECURUS: Dearest Amarissima, dry your eyes;
    Gently raise your head, so lifeless and sad.
    If you lost your life, I would end my own.   115
AMARISSIMA: For you, then, this bitter life I shall bear.
    But let us sing, you and I, because death,
    This monster,[9] ravished our happiness.
SECURUS & AMARISSIMA: (*Sing.*)
    All that is left is the sad voice
    With which I am able to cry,   120
    Lamenting the too-harsh absence,
    Alas, of him whom I so loved
    And I so cheerfully served,
    For I lost his happy presence.

SCENE III

AGAPE; AMARISSIMA; SECURUS.

AGAPE: I have lost him, the true comfort
Of my spirit, master of all shepherds.
I have lost him, the wisest of pastors,
And the gentlest that ever was on earth.
Thus he provided for and watched over
His ample flock, that he greatly treasured,
Defending and safeguarding it fairly.
Alas, I have lost the source of my good!
Before my eyes, death wrested him from me;
I was the last creature that he embraced![10]
What an adieu, how dearly I paid!
Words could not be found, no more can be said.
He spoke far better than the rest of us.
His body vanquished, his spirit triumphed
Over fear and death, and soared to heaven,
For whose loss I am nearly mad with anger.

AMARISSIMA: I am certain that his spirit
Reigns with Jesus Christ, his leader,
Exalting his divine essence.
Though his body is no longer,
The words of the Holy Spirit
Give him a new life in heaven.
    As long as he was hale and strong,
He wholly believed in his God,
His faith was his consolation,
And he died in this living faith
That led him to the shore most safe,
In which he communes with the Lord.

AGAPE: What sound is this, that far away I hear,
What song leaves me much-troubled and silent?
It is the voice of a woman, I fear,
Who is in great need of consolation.
You, gentle bird, that can so swiftly fly,
Go forth and counsel the unfeigning voice

125

130

135

140

145

150

155

That does not lightly or foolishly cry,
But in despair earnestly sings her woes.   160
AMARISSIMA: Alas! my body from its own
    Is exiled, for they had been bound
    From the days when we were infants.
    And my mind is also punished
    When it is no longer enriched   165
    By his, so replete with science.
      My mind and body, filled with pain,
    Are reduced to nought but laments.
    To weep is all that I can do.
    I cry in the woods and the plains;   170
    To heaven and earth I complain;
    I think of nothing but woe.
AGAPE: This voice draws me compellingly,
    For it is similar to mine,
    And the pain I feel within me   175
    Is quite like her very own.
    Her song appears to be old,[11]
    And yet the words are new;
    No matter whence the sweet voice calls,
    Its message I cannot eschew.   180
AMARISSIMA: Death, who so viciously mocked me
    By slaying my strength and my power,
    My sole refuge and defense,
    You were powerless to shatter
    My love, for it grows night and day,   185
    And increases my wretchedness.
      My pain is beyond common words,
    And is so difficult to bear
    That I am growing impatient.
    Thus I must speak of it no more,   190
    But think of joining him soon,
    Where he, by God's mercy, was sent.
AGAPE: Is it you, Amarissima?
    You, indeed, proving with your song
    That love and a faith that is strong   195
    Could never be weakened by time?
    Alas, death's evil design

         Is the object of your complaint.
         Thus I came to be by your side
         And help you carry the burden.   200
SECURUS: *(Sings.)*
         My saddened voice can only sing of grief,
         Thus my sorrow is ever increasing.
         Nothing that I see puts my mind at ease.
         With deep sighs, my heart is overflowing.
         I fear no ill and desire nothing.   205
         I can't bear it; oh Muse, bring tears to me.
         To nurture this weariness, everlasting,
         Is what I wish to do relentlessly.[12]
AMARISSIMA: Do stop, dear Securus, and let us hear
         A voice that brings back to my memory   210
         A dear shepherd, one that I recognize.
         For I am certain that it is Agape's.
         But if I knew where he was wandering,
         My tame starling I would despatch to him,[13]
         And I would ask if to us he would come   215
         To mourn noble Pan, resting in his tomb.
AGAPE: *(Sings.)* My desolation is so great[14]
         That deep in my heart it remains.
         I suffer numerous attacks
         Of the sadness that makes war   220
         Against my body and heart,
         So that, exhausted, I wither,
         Wishing I were among the dead
         For of this life I want no more.
AMARISSIMA: It is Agape: I know that sweet voice.   225
         Alas, it is he, I am quite certain.
         His pitiful song causes me to worry,
         Because, like me, he knows nothing but pain.
         Raise your voice high, Securus, for I think
         That he is near and will hear you calling.   230
SECURUS: Dear Agape, I beg of you, hasten
         Your weary steps, and come to me promptly.
AGAPE: Shepherd friend, from high above, with your shouts
         You call my name, but tell me what you want.
         You, who know me, do tell me who you are!   235

SECURUS: I am Securus, who all joy has lost,
          As you have, and if you promptly join us
          It will be a most charitable act.
AGAPE: Alas, Securus, your message is true;
          But what road should I take to be near you   240
          Without delay? You must advise me.
SECURUS: I must reveal to you the only way,
          And the road of the high cross is its name;[15]
          It is the path to the highest mountain.
AGAPE: Of the high cross? I know that road quite well,   245
          For oftentimes I have attempted it.
          My eyes see it and my heart loves it.
SECURUS: When I walked by your side on this journey,
          Near the high cross, alone, where you remained,
          You looked, though living, more dead than the dead. 250
AGAPE: May the Good Shepherd who took the appearance
          Of his flock, against all expcctations,
          Fill your heart with perfect satisfaction.[16]
SECURUS: I bid you welcome in this house of mine,
          Small and simple, and the season is cold,   255
          But I rejoice to greet you a thousandfold.
              I have many beds,
              And a blazing fire
              To keep us warm,
              Apples and chestnuts,   260
              Cheeses aplenty,
              And a good meadow.
              But do not presume
              To find very soon
              The great Pan's abode   265
              That was beautiful.
              Far from being so,
              So pristine and small
              But secure and clean
              Is my humble house.   270
              Away from danger,
              I shall shelter you
              In truth, and give you
              The best that I own.

I do live in peace,   275
With no fear of wolves.
We are not in need,
Happier at all times
Than those who by choice
Live in abundance.   280
But Amarissima is here
With me, and thus in her presence,
I beg of you to hold your tears,
For her suffering is intense.
AGAPE: Beware her cries as she sees me,   285
For if her eyes reveal her pain,
Such is the bond of misery
That in my eyes she will read mine.
SECURUS: Dear Agape, she has promised
That before you she would be calm.   290
AMARISSIMA: It is difficult among friends
To conceal one's deep emotions.
Seeing Agape, what should I do?
I feel his grief as he does mine,
But I must summon my courage   295
To sustain his own in this house.
SECURUS: Each of them is breaking the promise.
—Amarissima, such a greeting!
AMARISSIMA: When sadness meets with sadness,
It cannot hide its suffering.   300
SECURUS: Is this, Agape, the welcome
That you were to give without sighs?
AGAPE: Alas, I saw him in his tomb,
Our comfort and only joy.
SECURUS: And are you not fully aware   305
That man is born that he may die?
AMARISSIMA: Death has given me such despair
That from its depth I cannot rise.
SECURUS: No one may run to meet with death
Save on the fore-appointed day.   310
AGAPE: Must one see rotting in the earth
The man worthy of perfect love?
SECURUS: Let reason do within your heart

What time eventually will do.
AMARISSIMA: Yes, I complain, and I know why: 315
    Time will never undo my grief.
SECURUS: Alas, your body will not live
    With this unbearable burden.
AMARISSIMA: My sorrow, dear friend, will not cease,
    As long as blood flows in my veins.   320
SECURUS: Man must have the will to conquer
    His grief, listening to reason.
AGAPE: Reason has quite defeated me,
    As did my love everlasting.
SECURUS: But where are the laudable strength   325
    And constancy of the ancients?
AGAPE: Constancy! Only fickle hearts
    Can meet love with such resistance.
SECURUS: Trying to reason is fruitless,
    All I find in you is anger.   330
AMARISSIMA: Regrets, a withering desert,
    Regrets, abounding with sorrow!
SECURUS: Where are the strengh and the valor
    Of man, striving for victory?
AMARISSIMA: There is a reason for my woe: 335
    Forsaking it would offend me.
SECURUS: Lessons, philosophy, reason,
    Have lost here, it seems, all meaning.
AMARISSIMA: The more I contemplate my pain,
    The more I feel the bonds growing.   340
SECURUS: The foe is within us, rotting;[17]
    Let us not seek our demise.
AGAPE: Good, the most desirable good,
    Is for one to reach safe haven.
SECURUS: Well, then, I only beg of you   345
    That your voice be loudly heard
    Among the pitiful complaints.
AGAPE: Freely and gladly I expose
    My suffering.
AMARISSIMA: And I propose
    That earth and air be filled with mine.   350

(They sing together.)

I feel such torment and desolation,
Such is my bitter pain, biting and strong!
Oh! If I could but entertain the hope
That my death would end my tribulations,
And deliver me from this affliction!   355

SCENE IV

PARACLESIS; AMARISSIMA; AGAPE; SECURUS.

PARACLESIS: So much is too much and too much can't last.[18]
             Too much and too long have you lamented.
             The Good Shepherd, in his infinite grace,
             Sends me to the hearts he has tormented
             And with anguish in many ways tempted.   360
             But he takes at last pity on his sheep,
             Those whose heart can never be contented
             Unless it is sated with tender grief.
AMARISSIMA: But who are you, giving such a command
             To control the wretchedness of one's heart?   365
PARACLESIS: From the Good Shepherd I bring the command
             Of which, to you, I am the messenger.
             Although sadness has shut your hearts to me,
             I can put her to flight and shall enter,
             Regardless of what she may say or do,   370
             When his grace is bestowed upon you.
AGAPE: We would only see it as a blessing
        If our eyes could become a fountain.
PARACLESIS: But you must turn away from this mourning
             In obedience to the power most high,   375
             For I assure you that in the domain
             Of the Elysian Fields lives Pan the great,
             Liberated from suffering and pain,
             Who doesn't want his glory to be grieved.
AMARISSIMA: I doubt not that our Pan, so dear,   380

Was sent, having led a most pious life,
To the safe harbor; this, indeed, I know.
PARACLESIS: Then why are you still shedding bitter tears?
          Aren't you pleased to see his pious life
          Most justly adorned with the Kingly Crown?   385
AMARISSIMA: I am, but what I mourn is losing him,
          Or that death has not taken my body
          With his, making its wily deed perfect.
PARACLESIS: But if you would only listen to me,
          Soon, before your own eyes, you would see   390
          This Pan, whom you thought forever dead.
SECURUS: These words are hard for me to comprehend:
          That death should return what she has taken
          Would be quite contrary to her nature.
PARACLESIS: Here and now only can I announce   395
          That He who, from ashes, created man,
          Can raise him alive from his sepulchure.
AGAPE: Will this be when the Good Shepherd of all
          Loudly chimes the bells for the final call,
          Separating his sheep from the he-goats?[19]   400
AMARISSIMA: And until then, sheep, lambs, cows, and their calves
          Will suffer, forsaking dainty morsels
          And their fine wheaten bread to eat the coarse.
PARACLESIS: Pan is not dead, he lives more than ever.
          He is with Moses, Jacob, and David;   405
          They are in heaven speaking of their sheep.[20]
SECURUS: Pan alive! Such a thing could not occur,
          That this death, who had from us wrested him,
          Should bring him back to life! It is folly!
PARACLESIS: Pan is alive, to you I so repeat,   410
          In these beautiful and heavenly fields,
          Where endlessly, with his lyre, he sings.
AGAPE: I feel spellbound upon hearing you speak,
          And as I listen, my grief is waning.
          Paraclesis, you bewitched me, I think.   415
PARACLESIS: Your gentle Pan is in his true repose,
          And readily he goes, as would a spouse,
          To the Good Shepherd, as his true being.
AGAPE: I do recall that when he departed

His eyes and his voice most humbly pleaded   420
That the Good Shepherd's right hand be with him.
PARACLESIS: The Good Shepherd yielded to his request,
     Always ready for his own who seek help.
     He opened his arms to Pan, whom he keeps.
AMARISSIMA: I marvel at this befitting triumph,   425
     But I rue being here without him,
     And for so long, for which I grieve.
PARACLESIS: As the Almighty has willed it to be,
     Your own, to His will, you must surrender,
     And rejoice, for Pan is in great comfort.   430
AMARISSIMA: Alas! alas! no more can I see him
     Or gladly listen to all that he knew.
     Not seeing him, I like nothing I see.
PARACLESIS: Wouldn't you agree and feel contented,
     To increase his glory, not to see him   435
     For ten years, knowing him to be happy?
AMARISSIMA: Certainly, though I would be tormented
     With grief, and of seeing him quite tempted,
     But knowing him to be well would please me.
PARACLESIS: And yet you are aware that on this earth   440
     Men cannot be free from evil and war
     (For here all good is woven with evil),
     Exposed to the wind, the rain, and thunder;
     And then the mind ignorantly wanders
     Bringing forth in the heart many travails.   445
          The more a man can own,
          The more reasons he holds
          For worries and cares.
          The more honors he has,
          The less sure they are   450
          And the more he seeks.
          The more pleasure he has,
          The more he will desire
          To ever increase it.
          Every earthly good   455
          Vanishes as quickly
          As it has appeared.
          For Pan, by God's grace,

The good holds no cares;
'Tis good everlasting,   460
True honor free from grief.
Assured is the glory,
Forever free from shame.
Sweet pleasure with no fear,
Joy that is not a mask,   465
For all eternity,
And blissful happiness
That no necessity
Could ever endanger.
And whatever they say,   470
Pan is well, free from pain,
Alive and immortal,
Content and satisfied,
(As a perfect spirit)
He is, you must believe.   475
Now, be contented,
For before too long
With him you will be:
But still for a while
Through water and fire   480
You will have to go.
Do not lose patience
And your trust in God,
Rejoicing to see
Your beloved one   485
Asleep in the arms
Of the Good Shepherd.
When you are grieving
You awaken him
With your emotions: 490
Let him rest and sleep
By ending your cries
And lamentations.

SECURUS: Paraclesis, my faith grows with each word,
    For in you I see a true messenger,   495
    And in this faith my heart finds great comfort.

AGAPE: Now, since in his mansion he resides,

And as we believe that he is alive,
I am overwhelmed by your blessed words.
AMARISSIMA: Faith vows that in this fair temple he lives,   500
    Receiving abundant felicity:
        I gaze upon him,
    And in my mind, I can see him clearly.
    Love so powerful leads me to forget
        That it is in me,   505
    As I live in him; but as live he does
    I am alive now more than before.
        Gone is the shadow
    By which I have lived in this life so vain;[21]
    I am enraptured, and dead to the living: 510
        I have no yearning,
    And long for no other good but his own,
    By forsaking entirely my own,
        With the tender bond
    Of Charity that binds us into one,   515
    And we two have but one good in common.[22]
PARACLESIS: Since we have yielded to the Good Shepherd,
    And our will on earth to him we renounce,
    A far greater good from him I announce,
    As He sees deep into your very hearts: 520
    To you I promise, swear, and give my troth,
    Since you have for Him vowed abnegation
    Of your hearts, bodies, will, and intentions,
    And each of you has in Him total trust,
    He will be your good and loyal shepherd,   525
    Preserving you from all ills and dangers,
    From enemies, familiar or strangers,
    And everywhere He will be your shelter.
    Later, when He thinks it best to do so,
    With Pan, whom you so highly esteem,   530
    As shepherds and much-beloved children,
    He will gather all of you into one.
SECURUS: These are pleasant and most unusual words:
    Thus with a song it would be fair, I think,
    To give humble praise to the Good Shepherd,   535
    Thanking Him for this magnanimous gift.

AGAPE: I do not seek to spare myself,
        My weakened body, my mind, or voice:
        All this I give to Him without bounds,
        For we have much reason to give Him praise.   540
AMARISSIMA: My humble voice will accompany yours
        In this gaiety, as it had in sadness.
        However, my eyes will fill with tears,
        Feeling within me the divine mirth.
        Reason could at no time be my master,   545
        But the Almighty, who does and orders
        What is pleasing to Him, leads and guides us,
        And even pays for what He asked of us.
PARACLESIS: Now, let us all sing in harmony,
        Since the great Pan is living, and not dead.   550

(They sing.)

Si bona suscepimus de manu Domini, mala autem
Quare non sustineamus, sicut Domino placuit?
Ita factum est. Sit nomen Dei benedictum.[23]

NOTES TO *COMEDY ON THE PASSING OF THE KING*

1.   As a matter of protocol or to protect the dignity of the royal family,
      kings did not always attend the funeral services even for those closest
      to them. François did not attend services for his wife, his mother, or
      his children. It should be noted however that women were always
      present at such official functions, but Marguerite was either too shaken
      or too tired to travel to Paris for a ceremony that would have been
      exceedingly painful for her.

2.   Louise encouraged the use of mythological or pagan names to
      designate herself and her offspring. Their horoscopes, drawn for the

year 1510, include three unusual (colored) illustrations showing Louise as Latona, Marguerite as Diana, and François as Apollo.

3.   The masculine, Paraclete, has been altered to the feminine form, Paraclesis, and the feminine is used throughout this play (cf. lines 367, 495 and 519).

4.   The word "precursor" is all-important in this statement, since I wish to suggest that this work is not a traditional oratorio but is more closely related to this type of composition than to any other of the time. While scenery, costumes and action are not usually seen in modern oratorios, *The Harvard Dictionary of Music* (p. 516) indicates that "the earliest oratorios were performed. . . with scenery and costumes. In such a case, the more contemplative and less dramatic character of the libretto is the chief mark of distinction." It also indicates that by the mid-sixteenth century in Italy compositions of this type had an "extended libretto of religious or contemplative character" which included spoken narratives and recitatives with arias and choruses.

5.   Chastelain, Lemaire de Belges, Guillaume Crétin among others.

6.   Marguerite alludes to the repression of the Huguenots following the "Affaire des Placards."

7.   "He" refers to the king.

8.   Lines 49-54: This is the first stanza of the second *Chanson Spirituelle*, "Other thoughts written one month after the death of the king." Ten stanzas will be interpolated throughout this play: lines 63-68, 2nd stanza; 77-82, 3rd stanza; 119-24, 4th stanza; 141-52, 5th and 6th stanzas; 161-192, 7th-10th stanzas.

9.   The French "cymère," mythological she-monster.

10.   As mentioned by Saulnier, the king's end came rather rapidly and the Dauphin (Henri) was the last person to whom he spoke before his final confession.

11.   Georges Dottin remarks in his critical edition of the *Chansons Spirituelles* (Droz, Geneva, 1971), that the melody for this song is the famous fourth song of Clément Marot's *Adolescence Clémentine*, set to music in 1528 by Claudin de Sermisy. (*op. cit.*, p. 171).

12.   This is the melody of "Las! voulez-vous qu'une personne chante de qui le coeur ne ait que souspirer," also found in Estorg de Beaulieu's *Chrestienne Rejouyssance*.

    Line 208: The French "sans nulle excuse" means here "with no dispensation, as a self-imposed task."

13. The text suggests a trained pigeon, but the French "esclave estourneau" refers to a tame starling. The bird in question may be a "pigeon-étourneau," a small pigeon found in Europe whose markings closely resemble those of the starling.

14. The text indicates that this huitain is sung to the melody of "Je vous supplie, voyez comment / En amour je suys mal traicté." I have been unable to locate either this melody or the original lyrics.

15. This metaphor links the crossroad leading to the top of the mountain, and the way of the Cross, the only road to eternal salvation. Agape's answer (lines 245-47) addresses both meanings.

16. As indicated by Saulnier, the good shepherd who took the appearance of his sheep is God, who came among men as a man.

17. The French "fiens": filth, garbage, is frequently used by Marguerite to emphasize the corruption and the weakness of the flesh.

18. Lines 356-57: This repetition and alliteration is as unfortunate in French as its English equivalent. It is, however, a variation on an old French adage, "Trop est trop et trop n'est point bon," with which Marguerite was obviously familiar.

19. In the Scriptures, the sheep is a symbol of meekness, patience, and submission, all qualities required for salvation. The Good Shepherd will call his flock ("Multi sunt vocati...") and separate the sheep from the less docile goats.

20. Lines 403-05 echo a passage from *La Navire* in which the king tries to convince his sister that it is only since his death that he truly lives.

21. The less than euphonic alliteration of line 509 echoes that of Marguerite: "Dont j'ai vécu en cette vaine vie, Mais au vivant. . ."

22. Faith, Love and Charity are in turn allegorized in Amarissima's personal and somewhat enraptured meditation during the ongoing dialogue between Agape and Paraclesis.

23. Lines 551-53: "Shall we receive good at the hand of the Lord, and not receive evil, *if it pleased the Lord? Thus it was done.* Blessed be the name of God." (Job, II, 10 and I, 21, in this order.) It should be noted that "sicut Domino placuit" and "Ita factum est" are only found in the Latin texts and do not seem to have been translated in other languages of the Polyglot editions any more than in the Geneva Bible of 1560 or in later translations.

COMEDY OF MONT DE MARSAN

(Comédie de Mont de Marsan)

INTRODUCTION

Synopsis

A young and elegant woman proclaims her love for her own body. What she cannot see or touch is of no interest to her. A second woman, on her way to a pilgrimage, reproaches her: the soul is all that matters, and she boasts of the punishment she inflicts on her body to make certain that she earns eternal salvation. A third woman, to whom they submit their argument, blames both the ritualist and the worldly women, since the whole person is both physical and spiritual: abusing the body is as detrimental as neglecting the soul. She gives a Bible to each of the women, urging them to read it earnestly.

They are interrupted at this point by the love song and the laughter of a shepherdess, enraptured by the love of God, and they mistakenly assume that she neglects her sheep for the love of a shepherd. They question her and attempt to give her advice that she finds nonsensical and unneeded. Concluding that she is a fool, the three women leave her to her mystical ecstasy.

History and Comments

Saulnier, obviously intrigued by and delighted with this play, the longest of those included in the present volume, dedicates no less than thirty-three pages to it in his introduction, much of the material pertaining to critical analysis. Most of the other plays or farces were granted an average of a dozen pages, with the exception of *Most, Much, Little, Less*, which, because of its deliberate ambiguities, rated twenty-three. As could be expected, Saulnier scrutinizes Marguerite's religious beliefs and ideals in the light of the opening monologue of each of her four characters. He also studies their reactions to each other, individually at first, and later, temporarily, as an most unlikely trio nonplussed and therefore united by the presence of the fourth, whom they cannot understand.

With respect to the historical occasion of the play, we have been provided with an irrefutable clue: the author herself states that her play was "jouée le jour de Carême Prenant 1547" (1548 new style) at Mont de Marsan, that is to say that it was performed on Shrove Tuesday, February 15th, 1548. Prolific a writer as Marguerite may have been, it seems difficult to accept Saulnier's suggestion that this play of 1,013 lines was entirely written in January and February of 1548. I would suggest that it was written (among other works) during her husband's illness, which kept them at Pau, where they resided from late October 1547 until mid- or late January. One of her letters of early February indicates that she was by then in Mont de Marsan, where "they" would remain to celebrate Easter. It seems logical to assume that she had travelled there with her entourage (a far from easy journey of about seventy miles on mountain roads and crossings) for a Lenten retreat that could not have begun until late January but that lasted until late April, roughly two weeks after Shrove Tuesday. Writing a didactic play of such length in two to three weeks could constitute a remarkable feat of which Marguerite might have been capable, but it seems more likely that the *Comédie* was already written, and that the readings and rehearsals that are bound to have preceded its performance took place during that time.

Rather than ask *who* the characters are "in real life" and suggesting names for them, as has been done for various plays and particularly for her *Heptameron*, we should perhaps see *what* they represent: any attempt to give them an identity would limit and weaken the impact of Marguerite's message. Worldly is of course a well-to-do, carefree, and superficial woman whose sole preoccupation is the enjoyment of her material comfort, her clothes, her carefully studied physical appearance. She could easily be any royal mistress, any woman at court. We see her as utterly and blissfully vain, shallow, self-centered. Her task for each day consists in getting dressed and coiffed, then admiring herself and allowing others to gawk at her beauty. Her body is her all. What she does not see, what does not affect her at the time, is not worthy of her thoughts. When the second woman tells her that her flesh will rot, the thought of death only frightens her because it would destroy such a perfect and beloved body, and she therefore decides to enjoy life even more than in the past. When she is led on the path to conversion, not because of the stern and narrow-minded threats of Ritualist but because of the good and charitable advice of Wise, she is terrified of being found unworthy of salvation and hence of being damned. Wise then gently urges her to wish for divine grace with a pure and sincere heart, to live in accordance with this newly found desire for forgiveness, and to love God as she had once loved her body. Upon receiving the gift of a Bible, she eagerly promises to read it daily.

Without totally condemning her, Marguerite is somewhat more critical of the character of Ritualist who confuses true faith and ritual. This woman punishes her body on a daily basis with fasting and flagellation, spends hours on her knees in rote prayers recited for each hour of the day and each day of the month, orations that she meticulously counts by the hundreds, the more the better. She lulls herself into thinking that redemption is automatically earned by those who mechanically obey the traditional ritual. She is also prompt to condemn others, whom she sees as sinners doomed to damnation unless they follow her advice, although at the same time she seems to be totally unaware of her own transgressions. One cannot avoid drawing a parallel with the Roman Church or perhaps the Faculty of Theology of the University of Paris, which, holding both consulting and inquisitorial functions for the Parlement, put the fatal stamp of heresy on the slightest divergence from its own exegeses, and forbade the printing of French translations of the Bible. If we keep in mind that the Meaux Cénacle and those who sought a reform within the Roman Church lamented the ignorance of most priests, not to mention the spite expressed by the Inquisitor (in *The Inquisitor*) when he remarks that those who criticize him know the Bible better than he does, it is perhaps not by accident that we learn of Ritualist's ignorance of the Scriptures: when Wise gives her a Bible, she protests that she may not be able to read it or, if she reads it, to understand its language. She, at least, is willing to try.

Misguided as this character may be, Marguerite suggests that she is sincere but that she simply does not understand that the crucial element absent from her faith is that of trust in the true love of God. Numerous messages are sent in her direction, in the hope that she will hear them: grace is given to those who truly and wholly believe, those whose unquestioning faith causes them to accept divine grace as the ultimate and eternal gift, which cannot be purchased or bartered with memorized ritual. She must learn to establish a distinction between faith and dogma.

Clearly concerned and worried about the self-worshipping Worldly, but aware that this arrogant character naively reveals flaws and sins others recognize as transgressions, Wise reproves her more patiently than she does her devout and prudish accuser, Ritualist. She is severe with Ritualist, whose rigid "holier than thou" attitude and arbitrary condemnation of others constitute a moral judgment from which a true Christian should abstain.   Claiming one's estrangement from all sins is also, in the eyes of Wise, an example of sinful pride rather than a proof of virtue. But this character has thoroughly studied the Scriptures and their message, and hers is clear: to seek redemption by observing ritual is a denial of divine grace and makes a mockery of Christ's sacrifice.[1]

Far from threatening and preaching, Wise becomes the voice, nearly stilled but far from silenced, that Marguerite wants to be heard.   It is an echo of the voices of Briçonnet, of Lefèvre d'Etaples, of Berquin, of Dolet, even of Marot, all conveying a similar message, that of a simple return to the reading of the Scriptures in their most pristine translation, a denial of the self, and a trust in God rather than in institutions. In other words, Wise's task (or mission) is to help the two women see the error of their respective excesses so that each will sense and find on her own what she was lacking, to create a harmonious whole.

It seems paradoxically clear at this point that both Worldly and Ritualist satirize the Roman Church. We can recognize in Worldly (as we had in Much) a mirror image of the Church's self-absorption, love of decorum, vain obsession with lavish attire and decorations, utter disregard of spiritual pursuits, and ignorance of the Scriptures. There is furthermore no denying that the character of the superstitious Ritualist curiously evokes the dogmatic elements of the Roman Church, its blind obedience to man-made laws and rules, its glorification of formulas and litanies, its tendency to indulge itself while condemning others, its lack of Christian charity, its error in attributing to itself the power of redemption, which is God's gift.

Reason is an important element in the life of Wise: she explains to her companions that the body is to be cared for because it is simply entrusted to us; the soul is to be kept pure. Moderation, measure, love for others, wisdom, and learning are key words. There is very little doubt that she is at least in part the voice of Marguerite's evangelism, of an evangelical voice reduced if not defeated by those in power, but not totally silenced: the Bible still shows the way for the true believer. The Scriptures may no longer be read aloud in French, but their message, which cannot be denied by mere men, brings solace to those who read or hear it and to those whose heart is filled with the love of God.

The Shepherdess, Enraptured by the Love of God, is not given a Bible. Indeed, she would have very little use for it: she cannot read and has no desire to learn. Not only does she scorn all material possessions, but, revealing the innocence of a trusting child, she does not ask herself (or anyone else) questions about redemption. Hence, the Scriptures are and will always be of no interest whatsoever to her. Saulnier sees in her a clear rebuttal of Calvin, whose sharp criticism of Marguerite's protégés Pocque and Quintin, among others, had deeply offended her.[2]

In this play, the Shepherdess experiences a total and joyful union with God, and her somewhat erotic songs suggest a rapture that is physical as well as spiritual. Saulnier stresses that Calvin sternly rejected this type of "ravishment" because it separates the believer from his consciousness as a moral being (and thus affects his behavior). Marguerite shows this character as a totally pure and child-like creature who, precisely because she is possessed by the love of God, is incapable of behaving in an immoral manner.

We have already met a few characters who resemble this girl: the maid in the first play, the children in *The Inquisitor*, Little and Less. But substantial differences should be noted: the maid is an active instrument of conversion; so are the children, who are nevertheless witty and thoroughly versed in the Scriptures; although Little and Less seem oblivious to the hardship of cold and hunger, they are extremely cautious in their dealings with the other two men, whom they attempt in vain to lead to conversion. The Shepherdess is unique inasmuch as she does not care about what the other three women think or do, and has no desire to change them. She speaks when she wishes and says only as much as she wants. Having accepted the gift of divine grace, blissfully happy, oblivious of the physical world, its traditions, its rites, she is at peace with herself. Instead of reciting learned prayers, she babbles, sings love songs to her beloved, and laughs with joy. She does not rise to greet the three ladies when they walk near her, a breach of etiquette that is not lost on the miffed Ritualist, who, seeing it as additional proof that the poor girl is an absolute fool, reveals by the same token that she is perhaps excessively (and unchristianly) proud of her higher social status.

The Shepherdess also cares very little whether the sensual description of her consuming love (fire, exquisite pain, extreme pleasure, together with an incessant desire to be ever closer to her beloved) shocks these women. The concept of honor is irrelevant as far as she is concerned. For Wise, grace means union with the perfect friend, father, brother, child and spouse; for the Shepherdess, this mystical possession by divine grace, which has dissolved all notion of the flesh, is far more voluptuous and real.

Does she represent a mystic Marguerite as the end of her life comes near? Saulnier seems more convinced of it than I am willing to be. Indeed, one may see in Rabelais's prefatory *dizain* to his *Tiers Livre* dedicated "To the Spirit of the Queen of Navarre" an indication that she was lost in mystical meditations:

> Abstract Spirit, enraptured, ecstatic,
> Which, dwelling in Heaven, from whence you came,
> Have deserted your host and your servant,
> That assenting body of yours, which spurns itself
> Upon your command, in this life's journey,
> Isolated, indifferent and impassive,
> Would you not leave, if for but a moment,
> Your so divine and eternal abode
> Only to look at this, the third story
> Of Pantagruel's joyous adventures?[3]

Let us keep in mind that we are dealing with a master of the double entendre. Rabelais's poem may be a tongue-in-cheek allusion to Calvin's *Libertins Spirituels* pamphlet published the previous year; it may be expressing genuine concern, if, indeed, she had turned entirely to a personal religious quest. I am rather of the opinion that, paying homage to her lifelong efforts to shelter and protect "dissenting" authors, and sensing her discouragement, he invites her (who had generously protected him) to read between the lines of this, his third book, but also quite significantly *the first published under his own name*. What is certain is that if, from February to December of 1546, Marguerite had withdrawn from public life, she had done so for political rather than religious reasons.

This mystic ecstasy that she describes so well may have been what Marguerite herself sought to achieve. It represents the third and ultimate step in the Christian progress toward grace (Gratia Praeveniens, Gratia Excitans Atque Adjuvans, and finally Libere Assentiendo et Cooperando), but it is clear that it was for her an ideal rather than a reality. In other words, our author is too wise and far too close to earth to dismiss the reading of the Scriptures and to anticipate a rapture such as that of the Shepherdess. Her aim was both didactic and moral when she wrote this satirical play, and thus she leaves the door to redemption open for the two characters with whom she has the least in common, whatever they symbolize. Since Lent was to begin the day after the representation, she was allowed to entertain, but was also duty-bound to inspire, her audience. Thus, while a few scenes are quite amusing, the irony is gentle and the mood remains compassionate.

Except for the costumes—some of which had to be simply elegant for one, extravagantly lavish for another, and most traditional for the pilgrim and the Shepherdess—this was a very simple production. No elaborate decor, no backdrop, no multi-level stage were needed: a bucolic setting with perhaps a tree for the seated Shepherdess and a road or a path on which the other three women strolled would have sufficed.

In this lyrically and psychologically complex play, most dialogues are written in decasyllabic ten-line stanzas with only a few octosyllabic eight-line stanzas ("square stanzas" in both cases), but songs and various admonitions by the three women are hexasyllabic or pentasyllabic sizains. As the inspiration moves her, the Shepherdess will speak in lines of five, six, seven, eight, or ten syllables. When she joins the others in an attempt at some form of organized dialogue, there follows over two hundred lines of regular octosyllables, but finally communication disintegrates between the three women and the girl, and she returns to an irregular pattern of four-, five-, six-, and eight-syllable lines. Due to their solemnity, the last four lines are regular octosyllables.

In this play, more than in any other, Marguerite shows the value of silence as a rhetorical device. The Shepherdess uses a silence of prudence by refusing to answer questions, a silence of artifice by using songs or parts of songs to confuse or hold at bay those who annoy her, and a contrived form of silence by making the women ask questions for information that she truly does not want to give, causing them to reveal their own thoughts. When the lack of comprehension of her companions makes their remarks and their advice appear inane, and when she feels that further conversation would be superfluous, she withdraws in a silence of resignation. However, what is unique in this play is the unexpected, effective, and deeply moving use of silence at the end of a beseeching and yearning poem spoken or sung by the Shepherdess. This long silence, indicated by a blank line in the text, is a daring and eloquent symbol of divine grace felt on stage. This silence is a sudden illumination from God, a silent message of light or fire to the chosen and ecstatic soul. In the next four lines the Shepherdess seems to have lost all contact with the physical world. In a state of grace, she sings her serene and adoring paean of submission to God.

Marguerite amply proves in this work that she had indeed refined and finely tuned her skill as a playwright. This thoroughly polished work is probably the best of her plays.

COMEDY OF MONT DE MARSAN

(Comédie de Mont de Marsan)

Played at Mont de Marsan
On Shrove Tuesday
Of the year one thousand five hundred and forty-seven[4]

With four women, that is to say:

Worldly
Ritualist
Wise
Enraptured by the Love of God, a Shepherdess

SCENE I

WORLDLY.

WORLDLY: I love my body; do you ask me
Because it's pleasant and fair, I see it.
As to my soul that is hidden inside,
Neither my eye nor my hand can touch it.
To have none or one that I cannot see   5
Is all the same, and doesn't trouble me.
A soul may be soul to him who seeks it;
My body is flesh, I keenly feel it.
If it is in pain, I am much aggrieved,
And if it is well, I am satisfied.   10
    I decorate it,
Dress and adorn it
With gold ornaments.

Colored and painted,
I contemplate it   15
At every moment.
  And keeping it whole
Is my only goal
So that it may live.
Of melancholy   20
And of malady
  For it, I much fear.
For it I seek joy,
For it I avoid
What is unpleasant.   25
For it, fame and goods
I hunt and I hound
To keep it content.
  And all the beauty
That the eyes may see   30
I give to the heart
Till it is sated:
All this I will hear
But will love no one.
  Thus my sole intent   35
Is but to guide it
To pure enjoyment;
For the few demands
That it makes on me
I make it happy.   40

SCENE II

RITUALIST; WORLDLY

RITUALIST: (*She sings.*)
          I am on a long voyage,
          Pure of heart and with courage:
          'Tis a holy pilgrimage
          For Mary and her infant,

Whom from evil and damage   45
The true pilgrim does defend.
  (*Then she speaks.*)
The long journey has badly worn my feet,
And my poor body is so much aggrieved
That I grievously ache from head to toe,
But once I have felt pain and suffering   50
Deep in my heart I should find it pleasing,
For I shall earn from it ample rewards.
I feel so glad when my prayers are said,
And thrice my rosary's fifty Ave's.[5]
This one of mine comes from the Hermits' Mount;[6] 55
Many who have recited it were saved.
    When I pray, I seek help
    From the blessed Bridgette,
    Who had revelation
    Of the extreme torment   60
    Suffered, as was decreed,
    By Christ in his passion.
    To all Saints, orations
    I have, for all seasons,
    Giving me protection   65
    From all dangers and ills,
    And from cares and travails
    That I might encounter.
    And then last but not least
Is my nine-day vigil.   70
See these tapers, so fine:
When all nine are burning
And I can see their flame
Go up toward heaven,
    I know that my prayer   75
Will not be cast aside,
And that it was received.
Of the best, that are white,
I keep three for Sunday,
For which I expect more.   80
    And thus to save my soul
With flame, light, and water,

I shall spare no effort.
When life has run its course
It is the blessed soul   85
Whose body is revered.

WORLDLY: (*She sings*.)
Morning has risen, says the lark;
Rise, let us play in the meadow.
     (*Then, she speaks*.)
Well, then, since I am dressed and coiffed,
My labor is done for the day.   90
Is anyone better attired?
Is there a more perfect beauty?
And since with myself I am pleased,
Let all gossips talk if they dare.
Their mouths will ever be sullied,   95
And, what is worse, I do not care.

RITUALIST: O most blessed Virgin Mary,
So wildly does my poor heart beat!
She who should alas be sorry
And with her own self in conflict   100
Finds pleasure and satisfaction
Like a swine wallowing in mud
When she lauds and glorifies sin
With her laziness; it's most odd![7]

WORLDLY: But where goes this pilgrim woman   105
Who appears so weak and weary?

RITUALIST: On the road that I have chosen
There is no room for vanity.

WORLDLY: You lower your head most humbly
And must see yourself free from sin.   110

RITUALIST: It is for you, scoffing magpie,
Unseemly to hold yours so high.

WORLDLY: My head I do raise,
And to all I show
My body so fair.   115
Virtuous and good,
It is thought by all
As good company.

RITUALIST: This body of yours

<pre>
                   You value too high;   120
                   It is but carrion,
                   And it has to die:
                   We must suffer death,
                   Our snout's last groan.
WORLDLY: No, my fair green eyes   125
                   Cannot become food
                   For worms in the ground.
RITUALIST: You cannot endure;
                   Die you must, my dear,
                   Nothing is more sure.   130
WORLDLY: This too-willful death
                   Would not dare take me,
                   So young and so fair.
RITUALIST: But her mighty hand
                   No one, weak or strong,   135
                   Can hope to defy.
WORLDLY: This thought I reject.
                   My days will be spent
                   Free from such torment
                   While I am still young.   140
                   Old age in due time
                   With my death will end.
RITUALIST: Death has no season
                   And is not hindered,
                   By power or youth.   145
                   Sudden she'll take you.
                   Thus it is not sage
                   To count on old age.
WORLDLY: Well, indeed, if to-morrow I must die,
         Unbridled, free, I shall be hastening   150
         To all pleasures, sleeping, eating, drinking;
         Each moment will be filled with such delight
         That my life will be complete and perfect
         Before the day of the lady so black.
RITUALIST: No, no, my dear, there is a better way: 155
           For true pleasure you must suffer and pine
           By forsaking for your soul your body.
           Each day I kill mine and kill it again,
</pre>

And to earn paradise, for which I strive,
I spare no effort while I am alive.   160

SCENE III

WISE; RITUALIST; WORDLY

WISE: God granted to man a gift most splendid
By giving him reason, yea, so he did,
As to an angel. Isn't this gift fair?
Since he has reason, he gathers and counts,
Loves and knows virtues and gives them a name.   165
Because of reason, he is unlike beasts;
God placed high his eyes and his head
So that he may see what is above him.
The beast, below him, is bound to the earth
And to man, from whom it draws its strength.   170
    Man, with reasoning,
    Becomes most pleasing
    To God and to men.
    God he trusts, adores,
    Lauds, prays, and honors,   175
    As is his bidding.
    When needed, his hand
    He gladly extends
    To help his neighbor.
    He pays what he owes,   180
    And with joy follows
    The path of honor.

RITUALIST: Lo, my dear, this woman's discourse
Is greatly different from yours.
She seems quite at peace with herself.   185
Let us hear what she has to say.

WORLDLY: Yea, let us go to her promptly
And tell her why we disagree.
By looking at her, one can see
That she knows prose and poetry.[8]   190

WISE: I see two women coming near
             Who are of diverse opinion.
             I must hear of their quandary.
RITUALIST: May the Lord's blessings, my lady,
             Be upon you today!
WISE: Gramercy!   195
             And, ladies, may they be with you!
WORLDLY: To end our anxiety,
             In great haste we appeal to you.
RITUALIST: As soon as you appeared, Madame,
             And from afar, we ascertained   200
             That you can lift our burden,
             If you share with us your wisdom.
WISE: Do speak, for I am confident
             That if you can elucidate
             The causes of your argument,   205
             I will arbitrate your debate.
WORLDLY: I am corporeal, my lady,
             And I appreciate my body.
             I do not think beyond this life.
             I want to live long and fully,   210
             At ease, but quite respectably,
             In joyful pastimes, games and balls.
             I love my body, that is all:
             It is my friend, my progeny,
             My all, my God, and my idol.   215
WISE: This love is far too physical,
             And if you do not soon make amends,
             Such love will cause you to go mad.
RITUALIST: With her, Madame, I am at odds,
             For nought is dearer than my soul;   220
             All I want is its salvation.
             And thus, to make it clean and pure,
             Physical pain I must endure
             To better prove my devotion.
WISE: To save your soul! Alas, my dear,   225
             It has no greater enemy
             Than your misguided vainglory.
RITUALIST: What? Is it evil to defeat

           One's body for the soul's profit,
           If I may ask you, my lady?   230
WISE: But if your body is destroyed
           Before your soul is taught virtue,
           The whole endeavor is undone.
RITUALIST: What is this? Is it not worthy
           To defeat a sullied body   235
           With fasting, saying my prayers,
           By wearing a hair shirt daily,
           And with flagellations, always;
           Weeping, living solitary,
           Worshipping on bare knees in church,   240
           Fasting to edify others,
           Murmuring prayers endlessly?
WISE: God placed your body on this earth;
           You may not wage war against it,
           An act contrary to the Lord.   245
           Often, meaning well, one may lapse,
           Atoning for a broken glass,
           Or for having enjoyed a game.
WORLDLY: This, Madam, is not what I feel,
           For I do prefer a good meal   250
           To all of the fastings in Lent.
           I do not abuse my body,
           For I keep it healthy and free.
           As you can see, I love only myself.
WISE: True love for yourself this is not,   255
           For you, as your own self, are nought,
           If you mention but your body.
WORLDLY: My body, that I touch, is nought?
           Have I not two eyes and a mouth?
           I dare say, you speak most strangely.   260
WISE: You have a body, I agree,
           But it is made of mud and clay.
           Indeed, that body is not man.
WORLDLY: Man is not that which I can see
           And that my hand can touch and feel?   265
           I can't understand this at all.
WISE: The body without the soul

Is but a short-lived mass, or dust.
Alone it neither eats nor drinks.
A heap of matter, hard or soft,   270
It has no sight, hearing or speech.
Is this not true? Do answer me.

WORLDLY: My body without my soul
I haven't seen, and cannot say
If it can eat, speak, see, or hear.   275
But I feel it hear, see, and speak,
Smell, touch, and obey its nature,
One day sad, another happy.

WISE: The body neither speaks nor sees,
But you are deceived by the flesh   280
That makes you believe that it does.
It is only the player's flute,
But the sweet voice that comes from it
Is not that of his mortal flesh.

WORLDLY: But who sees with my very eyes,   285
And who, with my mouth, speaks and drinks,
But me, with this body of mine?

WISE: The body is only a mask
Worn by your soul, so do not ask,
For it is clear if you hear this: 290
When your body sleeps and slumbers,
Your soul, awake and forever aware,
Animates your body with dreams.
The immortal soul is within you,
And it must become the guardian   295
Of your body, true mask or not.
The soul is the only mover;
The body is its instrument,
To perform and do its bidding.
But when death that instrument breaks,   300
Man is said to have passed away,
And the soul guides it no longer.
The body will soon putrify;
The eternal soul cannot die.
Forsake your body for your soul: 305
Dainty and fair though it may be,

               It will become foul and ugly,
               While the soul remains beautiful.
WORLDLY: But if the soul is separate
               From the body that adorns it,   310
               Must man prize it exclusively?
WISE: Indeed not, for the soul alone
               Is not man; it is the union
               Of the two that one may call man.
               Bodies without souls are corpses,   315
               Carrion to be eaten by worms,
               And have little to do with man.
               The soul by itself cannot see,
               And it has no power to act
               When it has no physical bond.   320
               But the soul to the body bound
               Is man: the two in company
               Are most perfectly united,
               And with this union life begins.
               But if the soul is snatched away,   325
               This means the death of the body.
WORLDLY: What you said does stand to reason,
               That man be the two together.
               And thus I want more than ever
               To keep my soul in my body,   330
               And I won't fail to provide it
               With all pleasures, I so promise.
WISE: No more should you be enamoured
               Of your body, but endeavor
               To sustain it judiciously.   335
               But you must also be watchful
               As to the virtue of your soul,
               Of which you must think constantly.
               A soul filled with guile and deceit
               Will lead the body to defeat,   340
               And be damned together with it.
               But the soul filled with innocence
               Leads the body to excellence,
               For it is nothing but its sheath.
               Good or evil they may both do,   345

Good or evil they may both feel
Forever, above or below.

WORLDLY: I greatly fear this punition;
        When I think of my damnation
        Everlasting, my heart fails me.   350
        I am, alas, much too worldly,
        Of so shallow stuff, and so vain,
        That I am well-nigh in despair.

WISE: The worst of all is to despair.
        Your heart must fervently desire   355
        The grace of its God and Father.

WORLDLY: But I, who loved nought but my flesh,
        Would not dare to go towards him,
        For in me I find only sin.

WISE: This is the moment to confess   360
        To the Almighty the sickness
        Of your heart, sullied by your sin.
        He defeats sin in victory,
        Expecting nought but the glory,
        And you will reap all the rewards.   365

WORLDLY: Alas! could I, so vile, believe
        That the All-merciful and Wise
        Would grant me such honor and good?

WISE: Believe you must, and fervently,
        Obey and do His bidding   370
        In His service with heart and works.

WORLDLY: I do not know where to begin:
        And I am already thinking
        Of the evil I must undo.

WISE: To hasten your deliverance   375
        Do take this book as a present:
        It is the Old Law and the New.[9]
        There you will find what you must do,
        And who can grant satisfaction
        To guide you to life eternal.[10]   380

WORLDLY: Since it pleases you to tell me,
        I want to read it constantly,
        Seeking in it my salvation.[11]

WISE: Ignorance, the mother of fools,

	Has a cure: knowledge and wisdom,	385
	Common sense, and understanding.	
RITUALIST:	The Lord be praised, who reclaimed	
	This poor woman, a misled fool.	
	What you did was commendable:	
	She was tumbling down helplessly	390
	Into the depth of the valley	
	Of perdition most damnable.	
WISE:	You, who judge her life so infect,	
	Do you think yourself more perfect	
	Than she? Is yours a better life?	395
RITUALIST:	Better, I cannot truly say,	
	But I would have gone far astray	
	If I had coveted her life.	
	I do not play, I do not dance,	
	I do not spend in abundance,	400
	As she seems to do night and day.	
WISE:	But is dancing the only sin?	
	Do examine your own thinking,	
	Far more dangerous than dancing.	
RITUALIST:	My only thought is to do good	405
	In deeds, in words, in demeanor,	
	To benefit me and all men.	
	I recite my hours daily;[12]	
	I do good works incessantly:	
	On this I build my salvation.	410
WISE:	Yet against her you pass judgement.	
RITUALIST:	But it is not a transgression:	
	I speak out of compassion.	
WISE:	If you could see your own error,	
	You would see yourself no longer	415
	As a judge of her condition.	
RITUALIST:	I'm burning with indignation:	
	My duty is to right the wrongs	
	Of my neighbor, whose sins I know.	
	If I ignore his wrong-doing,	420
	I have no way to reprove him.	
	What am I expected to do?	
WISE:	Magistrates have the just office	

<pre>
              To judge and to render justice;
              Through them the Lord governs the earth.   425
              But if your life is free from sin,
              Against her you may raise your hand,
              And cast the first stone, in good faith.[13]
RITUALIST: Sinless, indeed, I do not feel;
              This is why I have avoided   430
              With all my might all corruptions.
              I have forsaken adornments,
              Banquets, love, and entertainment,
              And live in bitter contrition.
WISE: But since a sinner you are still,   435
              A competent judge you can't be,
              Yet in great haste you judge others.
RITUALIST: I judge myself as a sinner,
              And I go astray. However,
              I am neither wanton nor a killer,   440
              For which I praise the Almighty.
              For Him I so rule[14] my body
              That it can barely endure.
              I beat it, I force it to fast,
              To walk on long pilgrimages,[15]   445
              And to abstain from all pleasures.
WISE: Have no hope to gain from all this:
              Whipping your body till it bleeds,
              Exposing your flesh to the fire;
              Because your heart is not happy,   450
              Brimming with love and charity,
              You will deceive the Lord with lies.
              But deep in your hearts He can see;
              He scorns all pain, gifts, and journeys
              That were not born of charity.   455
              As true God of love and mercy,
              He wants the heart to burn with fire
              Till it bursts with humility:
              For until it has been humbled,
              And by love to Him you feel bound,   460
              Your mumblings are of no avail;
              Unless you are with Him as one,
</pre>

And feel in yourself His presence,
Your frantic efforts are in vain.
Do you see this worldly woman   465
Who to do well made no attempt?
I say that in spite of her sins,
Of which she is fully aware,
She has, through humility, the power
To become the Lord's friend and spouse.   470
She knows Him who has forgiven,
And ingenuously loves Him,
Her heart burning with charity.
She is now closer to God
Than you, who presume to find Him   475
Through somnolent fidelity.

RITUALIST: Then God's law is abrogated:
Whoever goes backwards is ahead,
And whoever did right was wrong.
One should give free rein to nature,   480
Forsaking good works forever,
And follow the worst of the flawed.

WISE: Pride has put those words in your mouth.
I tell you that you must follow
The road of the Ten Commandments,   485
Be constantly good to others
And never omit your prayers,
Calling to mind His Testaments.
But if your heart has not been cleansed
Of pride, and is by it sullied,   490
I say that you have toiled in vain.
God only receives with delight
The merciful and pure of heart;
With all your heart you must love Him,[16]
But you, who pass judgement on sin   495
While your own heart is quite unclean,
I think that you are in great need
To first acquire the knowledge
To judge upon your own conscience,
Or God is far beyond your reach.   500

RITUALIST: May my tongue be consumed by flames

          If I confess carnal evil,
          I, who stayed the most chaste of all,
          Or call myself a murderer,
          Who struck or killed no one ever,   505
          But rather suffered many blows.
WISE: Friend, I cannot conceal from you
          That there is no worse adulteress
          Than she who, forsaking her spouse,
          Loves and follows his enemy,   510
          And under his power she yields
          And violates her sacred vows.
RITUALIST: My spouse I never abandoned,
          For his widow I have remained:
          I've followed no other but him.   515
WISE: The true spouse, the almighty God,
          Have you not been forsaking him,
          Relying upon another?
          In another you place your faith,
          In the hope of earning from it   520
          Your salvation, pleasure, honor.
          But He is the God most jealous:
          With any other friend or spouse
          He does not want to share your heart,
          For your heart must be wholly his.   525
          Your mind, your will, and your power,
          He alone must have and possess,[17]
          He will not accept as rivals
          Spouse, children, father or master:
          The heart to no one will He yield.   530
RITUALIST: Has God not granted permission
          To love our children and friends?
          If not, we would be worse than beasts.
WISE: If you love, as He has decreed,
          The Good Lord, when you beseech Him,   535
          You will come upon the answers.[18]
          For when you love Him perfectly,
          Your neighbor, in much like manner,
          You will love, seeing God in him.
          Thus you will love God in Highest,   540

<pre>
              And will also love your neighbor,
              Seeing God in him at all times.
RITUALIST: This is a most cruel doctrine.
WISE: Well, then, you must read these writings,
              Where the only truth can be found.[19]   545
RITUALIST: Madame, I am too ignorant
              To sing in such a high register;
              None of it would I understand.
WISE: Dismiss your fears and read, my friend,
              The Old and the New Testament,   550
              Deeded to you by your Father.
RITUALIST: This is for persons of learning,
              But for me, with little schooling,
              It would indeed not be proper.
WISE: If you flee from the remedy   555
              That can uproot your malady,
              The only cause, your death is near.[20]
RITUALIST: I do not feel any sickness,
              But consent to what you suggest.
WISE: You need to change altogether   560
              To be cured of this malady.
              No more may you be so eager
              To declare that you are healthy,
              But when at last this misery
              You begin to feel aplenty,   565
              Your full health you will recover.
RITUALIST: To please you, I want to read it.
WISE: 'Tis the mirror that enlightens
              Your hearts and then lays them open.
              I am gratified to see you   570
              Reading this book forever new,
              For by it you will be renewed.
</pre>

SCENE IV

SHEPHERDESS (ENRAPTURED BY THE LOVE OF GOD).

SHEPHERDESS: *(She sings.)*
 Alas! with love I pine...
 Alas! each day I die...[21]
 (Then she speaks.)
 Who lives by love has a most joyous heart, 575
 Who possesses love cannot want better,
 Who knows love has nothing more to learn,
 Who sees love has a smile in his eyes,
 Who is kissed by love knows true paradise,
 Who conquers love enjoys perfect power, 580
 Who loves love obeys a sacred law,
 Who is transported by love knows no pain,
 Who can embrace, hold and see love
 Is hallowed with the Lord's grace sovereign.
WORLDLY: Listen to this song![22]
RITUALIST: Listen to the words! 585
WISE: Ah! Won't that be the prattle of a fool?
SHEPHERDESS: *(She sings.)*
 La, la, la, la, la, la, la,
 Of such good cheer she appears
 When her friend is close to her,
 Shepherd for the shepherdess.[23] 590
WISE: From her voice and her demeanor,
 She is in love, assuredly.
WORLDLY: Let us pause and listen to her.
SHEPHERDESS: Love has done me wrong too often for words,
 But the perfect love that is in my heart 595
 Has brought me solace and keeps me alive;
 Because of it I sing and weep.[24]
WISE: Love is what causes her torment.
RITUALIST: Love is all she sings about.
WORLDLY: Let us greet her to make her speak. 600
WISE: To startle her would be unwise, I think.
 Let us approach slowly and gingerly.

SHEPHERDESS: (*She sings.*)
        Of love my heart can't be weary,
        For God made it in such a way
        That true love is what sustains it: 605
        Love is for it joy aplenty.[25]
WORLDLY: Let us greet her.
WISE: Well said!
RITUALIST: God be with you.
SHEPHERDESS: And may he be with you.
RITUALIST: We come to you
        On a visit to learn of what you do.
SHEPHERDESS: (*She sings.*)
        I watch my sheep and my ewes.   610
WORLDLY: What? Have you nothing else to do?[26]
WISE: Idleness is the root of all evil.
SHEPHERDESS: (*She sings.*)
        I do my spinning when God provides,
        I do my spinning, yea, yea.[27]
RITUALIST: But your song only speaks of love. .   615
WORLDLY: Alas, it is a too-deceitful god.
WISE: Indeed, it is cunning and can beguile.
SHEPHERDESS: (*She sings.*)
        Oh, shepherdess, my beloved,
        Love is what sustains me.[28]
RITUALIST: Love is dangerous, I agree.   620
SHEPHERDESS: (*She sings.*)
        Of love I live and love shall I.
WISE: You must be respected less for it.[29]
SHEPHERDESS: (*She sings.*)
        Those grumbling fools who speak evil of love
        Have never felt in their hearts its presence,
        And, I swear by God and on my conscience,   625
        Are much to blame when such joy they reprove.
WORLDLY: Love is a cunning enemy.
SHEPHERDESS: I love my beloved
        With love steadfast and true,
        As by him I am loved,   630
        And so I love him too.
WISE: A woman with understanding

Must think of love as damaging.[30]

SHEPHERDESS: (*She sings.*)
    Love at no season
    Is friend of reason. 635

RITUALIST: Since from love she eliminates reason
    She shows little care for her salvation.

WISE: She is going from bad to worse.

SHEPHERDESS: (*She sings.*)
    Let them speak, let them tell,
    Let him speak who so wants, 640
    Gossip who gossips wants;
    Love I shall who loves me.

WORLDLY: She feels no shame and has no fears.

WISE: For her, nothing but love matters.

RITUALIST: She does not know melancholy. 645

SHEPHERDESS: (*She sings.*)
    Pretty little flower, so fair,
    I know well that you can hear me,
    That you do love and await me.
      I have faith in you,
      To you I am bound. 650

WORLDLY: But what could make her so content?

SHEPHERDESS: (*She sings.*)
    Love, gentle, secure and pleasant.

RITUALIST: What keeps her in this love so beloved?

SHEPHERDESS: (*She sings.*)
    Of boundless pleasure the sweet memory.

WISE: This is a novel oddity. 655
    Pray tell what makes you so happy.

SHEPHERDESS: (*She sings.*)
    Loyal in my faith,
    To love until death.

WORLDLY: Is there no longing in your life?

SHEPHERDESS: (*She sings.*)
    To sing and to laugh is my life, 660
    With my beloved by my side.

RITUALIST: I dare not believe what I hear.

SHEPHERDESS: (*She sings.*)
    Alas! There is no sweeter thing. . .

WISE: I fail to discern what she does and sings.
SHEPHERDESS: (*She sings.*)
               Let her not understand! I do!   665
RITUALIST: Upon my faith, you are quite mad!
WORLDLY: And mad she must be thought to be![31]
SHEPHERDESS: (*She sings.*)
               Love, be my safeguard!
               What could befall me?[32]
WISE: Wretched, I think, is the woman   670
               Whose heart feels of love the torment.
SHEPHERDESS: (*She sings.*)
               Happy, I hold this flame
               With no wish to repent.
WORLDLY: Do open your heart, it is best,
               And to us reveal your secret.   675
WISE: The grief that is shared is lessened,
               But increases when kept hidden.
SHEPHERDESS: (*She sings.*)
               Blissful is the pain
               Of keeping secret
               An adoring flame   680
               That sets hearts ablaze.
RITUALIST: To conceal the truth is your loss:
               You must speak to us openly.
WISE: When your lover is far away,
               Do you sing for your enjoyment?[33]   685
SHEPHERDESS: (*She sings.*)
               Alas! One can easily see
               By the longing for his presence
               What anguish and what misery
               Can be felt because of absence.
WORLDLY: But now, as he is elsewhere,   690
               You must suffer much fear and care
               Because of your being apart.
SHEPHERDESS: (*She sings.*)
               You, who are not aware
               Of what true faith can be,
               Contented you would be   695
               If, as I do, you knew.

WISE: What? your heart forever enjoys
                 This emotion, present or not?
                 I no longer know what to say!
SHEPHERDESS: (*She sings.*)
                 I love him so, so, so,   700
                 I shall serve him always.
RITUALIST: You feel that nothing we can say
                 Will alter your song or your heart,
                 But in this aim we must go forth.
SHEPHERDESS: (*She sings.*)
                 I would sooner die than renounce my thoughts.   705
WORLDLY: Death will bring your acquaintance to an end.
WISE: As for me, I shall forsake it.[34]
SHEPHERDESS: (*She sings.*)
                 But even after I am dead,
                 My spirit will remember it.
RITUALIST: I bid you well, my dear, but think   710
                 That you are, above all, quite mad.
WORLDLY: Have you, for us, no other word?
                 On the subject of your lover,
                 Tell us a word, or perhaps two.
SHEPHERDESS: What might you want me to say?   715
                 You diagnosed my malady
                 Before even feeling my pulse.[35]
WISE: Well, as she shows good intentions
                 I want to approach her again.
                 Tell us who is, do not tarry,   720
                 The lover that you so cherish.
SHEPHERDESS: You, ladies, who so condemn love,
                 Should not ask of the one I love,
                 But I say that his perfection
                 Heaven and earth cannot contain.   725
WORLDLY: You love him so?
SHEPHERDESS: I must confess
                 That I might not love him enough.
WISE: Of love you only feel the flame,
                 If you wish for more than the pain.
SHEPHERDESS: I do not know what pain you feel,   730
                 But the sharpest and most burning

                 Is to me best and most pleasing.
WORLDLY: Alas, my dear, just as you do,
                 This fire so sweet I once knew,
                 Which I wholeheartedly repent.   735
SHEPHERDESS: So exquisite is the substance
                 Of this love, that the more ardent
                 Its fire, the more excellent.
                 Whoever has felt it flowing
                 Will not, for it, be repenting.   740
RITUALIST: Alas, without repentance,
                 Great contrition and penitence,
                 You travel on a fool's errand.
SHEPHERDESS: Those who keep their love in their hand
                 Or in their eyes can forsake it,   745
                 Opening their hand or closing
                 Their eyes; but those who feel it
                 In their heart cannot be absent
                 From it, even for an instant.
WISE: Your lack of sense and poor judgement   750
                 Cause you to trust your emotions,
                 That you consider perfection
                 What may be its worst opposite.
SHEPHERDESS: I know little, I must admit,
                 Except for love, and have no wish   755
                 But to see the one I cherish,
                 And I do not see him half-way.
WORLDLY: Is it love or the beloved?
SHEPHERDESS: One looks so much like the other
                 That my eyes see them together.   760
RITUALIST: She dreams, or else she is a dolt.
                 You need a fool's bauble far more
                 Than this shepherd's crook of yours.
SHEPHERDESS: I prefer a simple flower
                 That brings to me the remembrance   765
                 Of my beloved, than to perchance
                 Own a treasure of great value.[36]
WISE: Gold has little appeal for you.
SHEPHERDESS: I see its worth, no less, no more.
WORLDLY: Having none now, none before,   770

<pre>
                 You cannot know what it is worth.
SHEPHERDESS: Who knows no hunger, heat, or cold,
                 And lacks neither food nor clothing,
                 Of gold or silver has no need.
WORLDLY: Is there nothing that you desire?   775
SHEPHERDESS: I have what keeps me satisfied:
                 Others may well want to be rich,
                 But this, for me, I do not wish.
                 A simple lass, I have no needs;
                 When I see the diversity   780
                 Of stars, of flowers in the fields,
                 Joyfully, happy and singing,
                 I spend my days in sweet repose.
WISE: My dear, you were not brought
                 Upon this earth to be idle: 785
                 The commandment must be honored,
                 By which one must labor and toil.[37]
SHEPHERDESS: In such may he only indulge
                 Who cannot sleep or lie awake.
RITUALIST: But to one forever at rest,   790
                 No good can possibly occur.
SHEPHERDESS: Who waits for the good to occur[38]
                 Will not find it; who has found it
                 Has no need to labor for it.
                 Isn't it so?
RITUALIST: No; who has it   795
                 Has All: but do show me the man
                 Who feels that he wants for nothing.
SHEPHERDESS: Ah! He who has it seals his lips,
                 And does not breathe a word of it.
                 You will not hear him boast of it,   800
                 Nor will he give the slightest hint.
WISE: But yet from one's face one may see
                 Whether the heart is satisfied.
SHEPHERDESS: Too much is often made, I feel,
                 Of judging thoughts from appearance.   805
                 You, ladies, see me sing and dance,
                 And conclude that I am content.
WISE: No, I think of you as hare-brained,
</pre>

For you rejoice, not knowing why.
SHEPHERDESS: I must say that you judged me well,   810
For my joy I don't understand.
I rejoice and take great comfort,
But do not understand my joy.
WISE: Alas, I walked this road before,
But another must be taken.   815
SHEPHERDESS: What road would you suggest I take?
I live my days in obedience.
WISE: It is the great path of science,
That by all men must be valued.
SHEPHERDESS: But love is all I ever knew.   820
It is my science, my study,
And the path where, never weary,
I shall run as long as I live.[39]
RITUALIST: She is simple and too naive.
Nought she knows, nought she wants to know.   825
SHEPHERDESS: I do know what I want to have:
Of more science I have no need.
He is far who thinks to be near,
Who is near feels he is so far
That endlessly he calls for aid,   830
For fear that he loves too little.
WISE: There is no sense to this riddle.
I think that love has bewitched her,
Under the spell of a lover,
And she has truly lost her wit.   835
SHEPHERDESS: You speak of it, but I feel it,
Though not as deeply as I want,
For my desire knows no bounds
In its insatiable yearning.
RITUALIST: My dear, that one is more cunning   840
Than good, to whom you are so drawn.
SHEPHERDESS: I shall not say that you are wrong,
For your every word is true.
He is not a fool, nor irksome,
But finer and wiser than I:[40]   845
I must love him more than myself
For his far too pleasing deceit.

WISE: But you should be sad and displeased
               To be thus betrayed and deceived.
SHEPHERDESS: Alas, such joy I have received,   850
               Casting off reason and honor
               For him, that my heart surrendered
               Into his arms, in his power
               (No longer of itself aware),
               To think but of him night and day.[41]   855
WORLDLY: I once held a passion too great
               For my own body and myself;
               Now for this I feel much grief.
SHEPHERDESS: My body I simply ignore,
               For his, to which my heart is bound,   860
               Causes me to forget my own.
               His, so filled with noble virtue,
               I claim as my own, and is mine.
RITUALIST: My earthly shell I did not prize,
               I hated and tormented it,   865
               Seeking, from the pain, to increase
               The final reward for my soul.
SHEPHERDESS: Oh! May my soul perish and drown
               In this gentle and blissful sea
               Of love, where there is no anguish.[42]   870
               I feel no body, soul, or life,
               Though I do love, nor do I yearn
               For Heaven or even fear Hell:
               But may I be with my lover,
               Together, as one, forever!   875
WISE: There is no point in what she says.
               In truth we speak to her in vain.
               Let us do whatever we want,
               For she does not want to listen.
SHEPHERDESS: I am too ignorant to learn;   880
               And thus I only want to say
               And do what can make me merry,
               Avoiding the sad and dreary.
                    (*She sings.*)
               Ladies who hear me when I sing[43]
               And see me happily laughing,   885

I shall tell you of my delight,
Which I feel the need to explain.
Should I not be satisfied
When I have the good I desire?

WISE: As she begins to sing again,   890
Her countenance is an omen
That she does not want to amend.

WORLDLY: One should not expect common sense
Where the mind is found so wanting.

RITUALIST: But is it not most surprising   895
That body, soul, honor, and wealth,
She disdains for the happiness
Of love, of which she often speaks?

SHEPHERDESS: (*She sings.*)
The wind bloweth where it listeth. . .[44]

WISE: I marvel at love's great power,   900
Giving her such joyful comfort
That she neither grieves nor complains.

SHEPHERDESS: (*She sings.*)
Not all who try it can succeed.[45]

WORLDLY: If her love were not of this earth
We would have seen it in her face: 905
She would also have sermonized.

WISE: The love of the Lord makes man wise,
Prudent, of good and clear conscience,
A student of the good science,
From morning to night, day and night.   910

RITUALIST: What she knows too well is to sit,
For she did not rise to greet us.

WORLDLY: That she is a dolt is obvious;
A greater fool could not be found.

SHEPHERDESS: (*She sings.*)
Ho ho he he he on on on.[46]   915

WORLDLY: She laughs at us in mockery.

RITUALIST: Her brain is much like her bonnet,
That of an ignorant herder.

WISE: But far worse, a ewe who wanders,
And has forsaken her pastor.   920

SHEPHERDESS: (*She sings.*)
       I shall be ever so charming,
       He will be my only minion.[47]
WISE: These words are not worth an onion.
       Let us go forth, leaving her here.
WORLDLY: And as you advised, we shall read: 925
       I long for it, for we tarried.[48]
RITUALIST: Reading is what I ought to do,
       Time is wasted in idle talk.
SHEPHERDESS: (*She sings.*)
       Let me go, go, go,
       Let me go and play.   930
RITUALIST: This song of yours we cannot praise,
       Which, wishing you well, I regret.
WORLDLY: As for me, I leave malcontent.
SHEPHERDESS: (*She sings.*)
       Your love, so tepid and dormant,
       Does not understand His secret.   935
WISE: Of all her songs, she only sings
       A few words, and with neither rhyme
       Nor reason, she finishes none.
       There is not much sense in her head.
RITUALIST: She is truly mad or stupid,   940
       Or conceited, or obstinate.[49]
SHEPHERDESS: I see as unfortunate
       Her, who does not know of love,
       And the one, too delicate,
       Who fears to come to the point   945
       At which one's security
       Means blessed felicity.
WISE: Indeed! she calls unfortunate
       Whoever is not, as she is,
       In this deluge of love, drowning!   950
WORLDLY: To mock her would seem quite fitting!
RITUALIST: But, seeing her limitations,
       We must shed tears of compassion
       And pray that she be forgiven.
WISE: She may some day merit Heaven.   955
       Remember that you were like her:

Winter is most unlike Summer.[50]
But we must leave, for it is late.
SHEPHERDESS: Oh, Gentle love! Oh, gentle gaze,
   Like an arrow, piercing my heart!   960
     The one forsaken!
   The beloved, by me adored,
   The righteous so poorly honored,
     And unrecognized
   By him who is not beholden!   965
   One is said to be cloaked but is nude,
     The other, hidden.
   The humble sling that cracks the wall
   And the flint stone that is so hard,
     They call it mild.[51]   970
   And the wise, they call him a fool,
   As to Peter, they call him Paul,
     And thus everyone
   Speaks the language of the others,
   But my heart can only love one.[52]   975
     And I prattle on,
   Forsaking James and little John,
   Body, shirt, short vest and gown,
     People and clothes,
   Treasures and goods, fat sheep and ewes,   980
   Drinking, eating, bread, white or brown,
     Pleasure and health.
   For joy, I have no closer friend,
   Nor to him could I be more bound.
     Alas, I fear   985
   Not to love him with all my heart,
   Or to love him faintly, horror!
     If I loved enough,
   This love would grant the death I seek,
   But since I am alive, at best   990
     I do not love enough.
   My arms and legs would feel weary
   If by love they were tormented. . .
     No, stronger they would be,
   For love, with infinite power,   995

Can easily bring back the dead.
  Do strive and travail,
Love, so that you may give me death.
When by you I have been conquered,
  I shall be alive.   1000
For you, I want to feel giddy
Without ever being free.
  But you, oh love,
If it pleases you to call me,
May I endlessly be consumed.   1005
  Your fire in me
Will make of me a new being,
Raising me to strike me anew
  And your light so pure,
Filling my entire body,   1010
Will makc me, as as you are, weightless.

* * * * * * * * 53

Thou hath so done and I thank Thee.
'Tis the fate of the Shepherdess,
Who, having truly felt Thy love,
On this earth has no other cares.   1015

NOTES TO *COMEDY OF MONT DE MARSAN*

1. Paul's Epistle to the Galatians, particularly II:16, 17, 20, 21, and III:11-15.

2. His pamphlet of 1545 (reprinted in 1547) *Contre la Secte Phantastique et Furieuse des Libertins, qui se nomment spirituels* reveals that he no longer thought of Marguerite as a correligionist, if she had ever been one.

3. Rabelais: *Tiers Livre des faictz et dictz héroiques du noble Pantagruel. Composez par M. François Rabelais docteur en Medicine & Calloier des Isles Hieres.* Paris, 1546, (*Imprimatur*, signed by the king was dated September 19th, 1545). The non-rhyming translation of this poem is mine.

4. As is well-known, the year began at Easter, and Saulnier reminds us that we must read 1548 (new style) rather than 1547. Cappelli's *Chronology* indicates that Easter, the first day of the year 1548, was celebrated on April 1st. We can therefore accurately date the first (and probably last) performance of this play as having taken place on Tuesday, February 13th, 1548, the day preceding Ash Wednesday.

5. The French text indicates one hundred fifty Ave's. The rosary is composed of 50 beads, for the recitation of five decades of *Ave Marias* each preceded by a *Pater Noster* and followed by a *Gloria*.

6. Saulnier suggests, after Lefranc, that the Mont des Hermites is either Mont Carmel or the Mount of Our Lady of the Hermits at Einsiedeln.

7. Lines 97-104: I do not agree with Saulnier, who sees in this struggle that of the devout woman within herself. It would appear that she is, in fact, deeply shocked by the worldly woman's vanity and by her lack of concern for her soul. She laments what she sees as the other woman's future demise.

8. Prose and poetry are metaphors for the body and the soul, the subject of dissension between these two women.

9. The Old and the New Testaments.

10. Among various translations of the word "satisfaction," Cotgrave mentions "cleansing" and "purgation." He further describes a "satisfactionnaire" as "a preacher of satisfaction." This is the Catholic theory of atonement: according to the requirements of divine justice, God and man can not be reconciled until human guilt is punished or acceptable

satisfaction made, but Christ made such satisfaction by freely and vicariously suffering and dying.

11. Worldly shows the zeal exhibited by new converts in several of Marguerite's plays: she wants to read the Bible from cover to cover or from morning to night (an echo of Marguerite herself in *Prisons*), but Wise—instrument of her conversion—suggests moderation and common sense.

12. The hours are the seven prayers to be recited during the day: Laud and Matins, said together usually at dawn; Prime, the first of the daytime prayers, at 6:00 a.m.; Terce or Tierce, at the third hour of the day, 9:00 a.m.; Sext, at the sixth hour, noon; None, at the ninth hour, 3:00 p.m.; Vespers in the late afternoon or early evening, most likely at 6:00 p.m.; and Compline, just before retiring. Marguerite may be hinting that even though the woman also says her rosary three times a day in addition to this, she still finds time to watch others and criticize their actions.

13. John VIII: 7.

14. Although "doubte" is found in Saulnier's edition, I suggest that "dompte, donte" ("controlling or taming" in Cotgrave, and fairly similar in script form) should be substituted. "Doubter" seems illogical in this context.

15. Although she had accompanied her mother (who firmly believed in their value) on several pilgrimages, Marguerite often depicts them as exercises in futility as far as salvation is concerned.

16. Matthew V: 6 and 7.

17. "And thou shalt love the Lord thy God, with all thine heart and with all thy soul and with all thy might." Deuteronomy VI: 5.

18. "Ask and it shall be given you; seek and ye shall find. . ." Luke XI: 9.

19. She obviously gives Ritualist a Bible. We should keep in mind that symbolic as this gift may be, in view of the lack of education of the recipients these would have to be French translations of the Bible. The edict of February 3rd, 1526, forbidding all translations of the Scriptures into French had not only never been repealed but was strictly enforced by the Parlement of Paris.

20. Marguerite used a similar parable in *The Patient and the Cure*.

21. Lines 573-74: (also found in Chanson 28 of the *Chansons Spirituelles*) were culled from a XVth Century song: "Hélas je pers mes amours" (Saulnier).

22.   During the entire scene (lines 585-709) the Shepherdess either speaks or sings songs of varying meter with no particular rhyme pattern, but the women's commentaries are all in regular rhyming octosyllabic or decasyllabic lines.

23.   Lines 587-90: We must assume that the audience was familiar with this simple song, since its fourth line is indented as one would in a quotation, but so far neither the lyrics nor the melody have been identified.

24.   Lines 594-97: Her song paraphrases Chanson 45 of Marguerite's *Chansons Spirituelles* (text, p. 129; melody, p. 182).

25.   A very clear echo of *Chanson Spirituelle* 36. Saulnier found parts of this song as well as those of lines 623, 628, and 633 among those of Eustorg de Beaulieu. It was common practice (even in Geneva) to use secular melodies and, occasionally, verses in a religious context. Marguerite herself in her *Chansons Spirituelles* used the melodies of a few bawdy songs for her own purposes. That she knew these songs may suggest that life at Court was somewhat relaxed, at least part of the time, and that her youth had not been as austere as we have been given to understand.

26.   It is somewhat ironic that Worldly, whose only task had been to select her clothes, arrange her hair and don her hat, now seems shocked by the fact that the Shepherdess does nothing but watch her flock all day.

27.   Refrain of a popular song paraphrased in *Chanson Spirituelle* 37.

28.   Lines 618-19 and 621 are a paraphrase of *Chanson Spirituelle* 36.

29.   Ambiguous in French, as in English; English: both "devoir" and "must" can imply either probability or necessity. Yet it would be out of character for Wise to imply a moral obligation to withhold respect.

30.   Cf. the *Heptameron*: "Il faut fuir l'amour, qui detruit" (Oisille, 3rd tale); "Love, even virtuous, must be kept secret" (Parlamente, 70th tale); Ennasuitte also feels that love is a potentially damaging passion, of which one must be extremely wary. This is as well the belief of the first girl in the *Comedy for Four Women*. Of course, this is a moot question for the Shepherdess.

31.   An ambiguity in both languages: "She acts so strangely that this would be a logical explanation," or "We must believe that she is mad because this would be the only possible excuse for such outrageous behavior."

32.   Lines 668-69 are an echo of *Chanson Spirituelle* 44.

33.   Wise implies that the Shepherdess sings to make believe that she is happy or to convince herself that she is.

34. Saulnier suggests that "la" (translated here as "it") refers to the Shepherdess, and that Wise, tired of her non-answers, is ready to leave, ending this fruitless conversation. I believe that "la" refers to the worldly acquaintance that she will leave by choice. This seems to be confirmed by the next two lines.

35. The Shepherdess is at last engaging the women in conversation, instead of singing answers they do not comprehend, and from this moment on she will speak in eight- or ten-syllable lines with a regular rhyme pattern.

36. "The Law of Thy Mouth is better unto me than thousands of gold and silver" (Psalm 119: 72). Allusions to the Scriptures in this passage are too numerous to be listed.

37. A paraphrase of Genesis III: 19.

38. Lines 791 and 792 end with the same word, and Marguerite may thus indicate that the Shepherdess easily counters the other woman's arguments; she will do so again in lines 812 and 814, repeating word for word the other's remark in her reply.

39. Lines 820-23 echo *Chanson Spirituelle* 36.

40. The Shepherdess plays on the word "fin," which means both "cunning, devious", and "fine, good, subtle."

41. This very sensual description of her rapture is reminiscent of that of Ste Theresa of Avila. It is also an echo of *Chanson Spirituelle* 36.

42. Marguerite "borrows" Maurice Scève's metaphor on earthly love in the Prefatory Epistle to his translation of Juan de Flores's *Fiametta*. Whereas Scève expresses his fear that this "sea of love" may "drown" the lovers, it is precisely this loss of self in religious ecstasy that the Shepherdess welcomes. (Saulnier)

43. This seems to represent a turning point in this dialogue, as the Shepherdess begins singing again. It should be noted that even when she spoke in octosyllabic lines her language was less structured than that of the other women. Frequent enjambements and chevilles suggest what we may call an early example of stream of consciousness or interior monologue.

     Lines 884-958: The women speak in octosyllabic lines (most usually in a regular rhyme scheme), but the new songs of the Shepherdess will continue to vary greatly in rhyme and metre.

44. "Autant en emporte le vent" is the refrain in Marguerite's 5th *Chanson Spirituelle*. Quite popular in the second half of the XVth century, it is found in Villon's *Ballade en vieil langage francoys* and in various

volumes of French songs of the early XVIth century. Marguerite's 5th Chanson was reprinted in the *First Book of Psalms and songs written in French & put to music by various Authors,* Paris, 1552 (cf. *Chansons Spirituelles*, pp. 15, 144-45, 172). It was also included in the *Chansonnier Protestant* of 1555.

45. This is the refrain of *Chanson Spirituelle* 29.

46. We must assume that she is humming a melody, keeping the words to herself. Not only are words unnecessary in her relationship with God, but all traditional forms of communication with the women have ended as far as she is concerned.

47. Echo of *Chanson Spirituelle* 38.

48. Wise gave each of them (except the Shepherdess, of course) a Bible and told them to read it daily.

49. In the theological sense of the word, "obstinate" means "incorrigible," and refers to the unrepentant sinner.

50. "She may be more reasonable and virtuous in her old age than she is now."

51. Although Saulnier suggests the word refers to "the scaffolding that surrounds a building in construction" (followed by two question marks to indicate his doubts as to this interpretation, I am not convinced. I would propose that the word refers to a slingshot. This also appears more compatible with the text, not to mention the fact that Cotgrave only gives "flint" as a translation for the word "caillou," thus confirming the ability of this weapon to do extensive damage and literally "part a wall" (part le mur) rather than surround it.

52. Only one language, that of love.

53. This is the most important moment in the play, the moment of silence, an illumination from God translated by a silence of ecstasy, when the soul is temporarily a separate entity from the body.

COMEDY ON PERFECT LOVE

(Comédie du Parfait Amant)

INTRODUCTION

Synopsis

For centuries, an extremely old woman has wandered the world over to give a crown of flowers symbolizing perfect love to the one person worthy of wearing it. Exhausted and discouraged because none of the eager candidates can truthfully receive such a noble award, she gives an audience to three young women who claim the crown. But fickle, selfish, or unfaithful, they fail the test. A young man chooses his beloved for this honor which she refuses, insisting that he should receive it. Jeanne d'Albret and Antoine de Vendôme are invited to decide which of those two deserves the crown.

History and Comments

Saulnier dismisses this play as "nothing but courtly entertainment," and "a posy offered by an aging to woman to her young guests." One must concede that it was perhaps written too fast, during the Spring of 1549, to be performed once, most likely on the occasion of Jeanne d'Albret's visit, and never revised or edited by its author. The voyage of Marguerite's daughter to Navarre may have been dictated by protocol to introduce her husband, Antoine de Vendôme, to her future subjects. Jeanne had lived in France most of her youth and the king of France had not allowed her to travel to Navarre after her (non-consummated) marriage to the Duke of Clèves had finally been annulled by the Pope. However, in choosing to stay with her mother longer than a political engagement required, Jeanne clearly showed to those who declared them to have been at odds for years that she had not simply come to pay her respects to her royal parents and that her journey was a personal and private visit as well.

That Marguerite had dreamed of a different spouse for her daughter is well known, but François had always been irrevocably opposed to the desired union with Philip, future king of Spain, and so was Henri II. In 1548, much to her chagrin, her nephew the king ordered that Jeanne be married to Antoine. The distressed parents of the bride were openly and uncharitably mocked at the wedding, but in all fairness one must admit that Jeanne seems to have been genuinely smitten with her designated spouse.

Marguerite pragmatically submitted to a decision that she had no power to contest, but is bound to have noticed Jeanne's happiness, and she light-heartedly narrated in her *Heptameron* an amusing *quid pro quo* which took place soon after the ceremony. She was naturally elated by the young couple's visit a few months after the wedding, and because life in Navarre was less animated than that of the French Court, she decided that a short play would serve well, both to amuse and to honor her guests.

The theme of this comedy—"What is perfect love?"—is developed from its most basic and obvious manifestations to the the greatest moral challenge it imposes on the lover. Thus when the old woman denies the three women's requests, she dejectedly explains to each of them why they failed:

First, true love demands faithfulness whether the beloved is absent or not. A lengthy separation is the crucial test, for it must not affect or alter in any way the intensity of the lovers' devotion to one another. More important yet, it imposes the most rigid standards of fidelity, even if one of the lovers betrays the other. In other words, love thus has become an entity of its own, to be protected, cherished and revered: the lovers only become the instrument of this enthralling spirit.

While these rigid criteria were to be obeyed, they still did not represent perfect love as Marguerite conceptualized it after reading Plato, or rather as she understood him from the writings of Ficino and through the eloquent statements of Castiglione's Bembo. She was at the time exploring and refining for the dialogues of the *Heptameron* this *topos* so close to her heart, and which she had already analyzed for the *Comedy for Four Women* and various other works. In all these, she shows many subtle nuances in the relationship between men and women, be it ideal love or ideal friendship (which closely ressembles it), but her concept of perfect love remains platonic. Ignoring if not excluding sexual possession, sustained by the "pure image" of the beloved, it transcends physical love and and rises beyond the intellect in its ultimate quest for beauty and virtue. It is an irresistible spiritual, almost divine, force by which the lover aspires to lose himself (or herself) in the image of the beloved, in total devotion and self-abnegation. This is clearly not what our elderly traveler has found during her lengthy and fruitless journey.

Having angrily sent the three girls away, the old woman, anxious to bring to an end her frustrating mission, invites a young man to claim the crown. He designates his loyal and virtuous beloved as the only one deserving to wear it, and in what must be an entertaining scene, the old woman follows him as he rushes toward the young woman. An overabundance of hyperbolic mutual praise ensues as each adamantly refuses the coveted award for the benefit of the other, thereby placing the old woman in a quandary. Unable to decide between these two ideal lovers, she turns to Jupiter and Juno and asks them to award the crown to one of them.

Juno "the Wise" and Jupiter were, of course, the guests of honor, Jeanne and Antoine, most likely seated in front of the stage. It is rather amusing to think that they were unexpectedly asked to solve the old woman's dilemma, to the great pleasure of the audience. One may easily imagine Antoine gallantly choosing the young woman and Jeanne congenially selecting the young man, unless they opted to have the two share this crown which neither would wear.

We shall not be as severe as was Saulnier in his evaluation of this work as a trifle, a "grandmotherly moral game in which sugary advice is offered to younger persons," but there is no denying that this comedy, probably the last one that she wrote, is not one of Marguerite's better efforts. Once again, the debate form is featured, a genre of which she was fond, though here it is quite brief and written entirely in easily memorized decasyllabic rhymed couplets. Its performance required only a simple decor: in the background, a meadow where the young woman stands alone, and a road (or a clearing) where the old woman, the three girls and the man gather.

In a short play whose sole purpose is to entertain a courtly audience, there is no need for dramatically effective techniques or for an impressive display of eloquence leading to a moral lesson. Obviously, Marguerite's didactic soul could not resist including a few hints on mutual respect and faithfulness that would not fall on deaf ears, and more particularly on those of her straying husband. Although she condemned women whose revenge was retaliation, she repeatedly stressed how deeply she resented the casual attitude of many a husband (except her brother!) to his marriage vows.

We have already noted that, either to prove her versatility and her skill as a serious and dedicated author, or simply to leave for posterity a "sampler" of her better works, she selected for her *Marguerites de la Marguerite des Princesses* at least one example of every literary genre in which she had written. We may safely assume that, had this brief comedy been completed before 1547, she would not have counted it as one of her *Marguerites* unless she had revised it as she had the others, eliminating some of its flaws. We should perhaps also keep in mind that, written for a unique event of great sentimental importance (the long awaited reunion with her daughter), *Comedy On Perfect Love* represents a rare moment of light-hearted happiness and of pleasure experienced by the ailing queen of Navarre during her last year on earth. A posy it may be, but a charming one it is, and clearly meant to be enjoyed rather than admired.

COMEDY ON PERFECT LOVE[1]

(Comédie du Parfait Amant)

Woman   First Girl[2]
Man   Second Girl
                  Third Girl
                  Fourth Girl

SCENE I

WOMAN; FIRST GIRL; SECOND GIRL; THIRD GIRL.

WOMAN: Though for hundreds of years I have wandered,
Not one have I found to lift my burden.
One hundred times, traveling round this Earth,
Diligently, far and wide, I have searched. . .
Oh world, filled with evil and so fickle!   5
And yet I must proceed in this travail,
Darting to and fro, till at last is found
A person whose love is true perfection.
This task is beset with difficulties:
My days and all my efforts are wasted.   10

FIRST GIRL: If you would, My Lady, noble and wise,
Kindly tell us why, before our eyes,
You so grieve, we would with you humbly plead
Not to keep from us such affliction:
You would perchance find the consolation   15
That you seek? But tell us, we pray,
Why you must endure such adversity.
We wish we had the ability
To provide you with a swift remedy,
For we want to lessen your misery.   20

WOMAN: If you insist upon hearing this tale,
I have for many years and many moons,
Far and wide, carried this garland of blooms

To find the one, whether male or female,
Who, because of true love, pure and honest,   25
Will be judged most worthy of wearing it.
But I have uncovered such fickleness
That nowhere can I pause or end my quest.
FIRST GIRL: Ah! Good fortune has at last met with me!
For nowhere on this earth could there be   30
Another head more fit to wear this crown
Than my own!
WOMAN: No, no. It is not given
So easily: first I need to be sure
That you have truly obeyed all the rules.
FIRST GIRL: Yes indeed, for I do harbor a love   35
In which reign both virtue and chastity,
A love so perfect that it has no peer.
And thus, madame, with me you must agree.
Give it to me.
WOMAN: No, no, my dear, not yet.
I need to know—and please keep no secrets—   40
When this too perfect love of yours began.
FIRST GIRL: For a full year I have endured the pain.
WOMAN: 'Tis not enough. Have you felt the torment
Of his having been but one day absent?
FIRST GIRL: Certainly, madame. I suffered much grief   45
Not having seen him for nearly a week.
WOMAN: Has he never left for a long journey?
FIRST GIRL: He has, madame, for three months, certainly.
WOMAN: During that time, was he not forgotten?
Didn't the love that teases fickle hearts   50
Cause your singleness of heart to waver?
Didn't you wish to marry another?
FIRST GIRL: During those months, it is true, I aver,
I often saw others, honest and fair,
Whom I loved: but not of a love equal   55
To that for my friend, who has no rival.
WOMAN: Oh fickle heart, if three months of absence
Could overcome your constancy
And taint it with so much frivolity,
Of this garland you cannot be worthy!   60

SECOND GIRL: No, she is not, but I am, My Lady.
      My love has never changed and never will.
      For I have loved, and love, and love I shall,
      And my love for him never could be false.
WOMAN: Have you not the most perfect beloved?   65
SECOND GIRL: Indeed, the most perfect upon this earth.[3]
WOMAN: And he loves no one more than you, you say?
SECOND GIRL: No, dear Lady, he is staunch in his faith.
WOMAN: Then, why should you not love him most dearly,
      If he is your friend far more than his own?   70
      Has he ever been but one day absent?
      Tell me honestly your heart's sentiment.
SECOND GIRL: No, my Lady, I have for these two years
      Seen him daily and know him to be true.
WOMAN: But if he were for two long years absent,   75
      Would you love him as if he were present?
SECOND GIRL: Yea, for my love, intolerant and fierce,
      Would keep me from growing fickle or weak.
WOMAN: So, you have never been put to the test?
      I have not yet found the end of my quest.   80
SECOND GIRL: But it is mine, it does belong to me!
WOMAN: Who pines for it is far from having it:
      For you have not yet known all the torment,
      And you have felt nought but the contentment.
      Thus you have not yet won the noble crown: 85
      Your untried love calls for this decision.
THIRD GIRL: I agree: neither of them deserved it,
      But I do, for my torment is acute.
WOMAN: Tell me all about your love, my dear.
THIRD GIRL: I have cherished day and night for two years   90
      One so perfect that better can't be found.
      He has my word, and his he has proven.
      He is in love with me, and I with him.
      This is my weal, my stay, my peace of mind.
      He left for half a year, but this being apart   95
      Has weakened neither my love nor my heart.
      Thus, madame, give the crown to me forthwith.
WOMAN: Not so fast! my child, you are too hasty.
      And if he wanted to love another,

                     Would you, my dear, swallow a pill so bitter?   100
THIRD GIRL: Another? Alas, when I loved him so,
                     Honored and cherished above all others?
                     I would leave him if he dared betray me.
                     Oh! How weary of him I would be!
WOMAN: Listen! If you were intent on revenge,   105
                     What would you do?
THIRD GIRL: Me? Find another friend!
WOMAN: I should have known! Before she even sees
                     This evil take place, she breaks her promise,
                     Casting aside of love the mutual pledge.
                     For, once a vow is given and received,   110
                     It is to the soul eternally bound.
                     Be on your way, you much too fickle woman,
                     For you do not deserve this noble crown!
                     Your thoughts of a new friend arose too soon.
                     But I see a man, walking on this road,   115
                     And it is clear that his thoughts are morose.
                     —May the fulfillment of your desires
                     Be swiftly granted by the Almighty!
                     Might you not attempt to receive this crown,
                     Of which no person has yet been worthy?   120
MAN: I, madame? Why? And what is its power?
WOMAN: It will belong to the one
                     Whose heart will be filled with love, faithful and true.
MAN: It won't be mine, madame, I assure you!
                     But look in the meadows: there is the one   125
                     Object of my care and my devotion.
                     If a lover that is true and constant
                     Is to be awarded this fair garland,
                     'Tis she (and no other) who will be its owner.
WOMAN: To hear what she says, let us go to her.   130

SCENE II

MAN; FOURTH GIRL; WOMAN

MAN: May God preserve from evil one so true!
FOURTH GIRL: And for your virtue may God reward you!
               Do you see, walking to you, this lady?
               She's coming to meet you most eagerly,
               Having heard the praises of your good name,   135
               That shines so high among those of women
               For your supreme and constant loyalty.
WOMAN: Blessed be the time, the month, and the day
               When we met, if you help me give the crown
               Away, the reason for this tale of mine   140
               That must be told: it can only be given
               Where true constancy in love is proven.
FOURTH GIRL: Madame, seek no longer but hear my plea;
               Award the crown to him and not to me.
               I know him well and I can truly swear   145
               That his faithfulness is beyond compare.
MAN: Alas, madame, it is I she adored
               When a glance from her I dared not hope for,
               And she remained, during my long absence,
               Perfectly true.
WOMAN: Oh, happy acquaintance!   150
FOURTH GIRL: But, dear Lady, judge of the loyalty
               Of this gentle man, and his courtesy!
               A humble heart, magnanimous, flawless
               Can't be called valorous. Nevertheless,
               Because of his deeds and his far-known fame,   155
               He should bear of Mars the glorious name.
               Wherever he went—Oh rare quality!—
               He paid no heed to far greater beauties;
               Yet he, whose charm and grace are unequalled,
               Chose me, though plain, and finds me lovable.   160
MAN: For years, my remaining or my absence,
               On her love, madame, had no influence.
WOMAN: One of you two will win, you will agree,

Yet I know not which of you it must be:
And so to end my travail and my pain, 165
I beg you to let me show you the way
To Jupiter and his Juno the sage.
I shall speak of my venerable age;
They will hear of the peregrination
During which I suffered great vexation.[4] 170
And to whichever of you they confer
The wearing of this crown, the deserved honor,
I shall, with great eagerness, present it.

FOURTH GIRL: In good faith, madame, I shall not take it.

MAN: Neither shall I, for it is truly yours. 175

WOMAN: Let us go, then, and may the Great Power

Who created this world from nothingness
Grant wisdom to us all on this journey.[5]
For you, my Lord and My Lady, I pray
That your hearts from evil and care be free. 180
And may He always remain by your side.
You have seen and heard, I am satisfied,
What true love has said, resolved and decreed:
Thus, you can cause my wandering to cease.
Of the two, choose, prithee, upon whose head 185
To place this crown that I must humbly yield.

NOTES TO *COMEDY ON PERFECT LOVE*

1. Originally *Le Parfait Amant* (*The Perfect Lover*), but given the nature of the debate the above title seems preferable.

2. These four girls are unmarried young women, presumably in their teens or early twenties.

3. Saulnier points out the fact that in several of Marguerite's works the only perfect beloved is Christ, and that no mortal is worthy of being called "perfect." Second Girl clearly states that her beloved is the most perfect *on earth*, a very subtle but all-important nuance.

4. Again, this long-winded complaint reflects her long and frustrated quest (one thousand years!) and her zealous anticipation to have the crown taken off her hands.

5. We assume that at this point the old woman turns to the two guests of honor (Jeanne d'Albret and her husband Antoine), because she is now addressing them directly and with utmost respect. They are clearly called upon to take the crown from the old woman's hands and to place it on the head of Fourth Girl or that of Man.